1980s BUMPER Activity Book

1980s BUMPER Activity Book

52 GROWN-UP PROJECTS THAT LOOK BACK TO THE FUTURE

I ♥ MEL

PORTICO

By
Mel Elliott

First published in the United Kingdom in 2012 by
Portico Books
10 Southcombe Street
London
W14 0RA

An imprint of Anova Books Company Ltd

ISBN 978-19075-547-9-7

A CIP catalogue record for this book is available from the British Library.

10 9 8 7 6 5 4 3 2 1

Printed and bound by Toppan Leefung Printing Ltd, China

This book can be ordered direct from the publisher at
www.anovabooks.com

For more information about Mel why not visit
www.ilovemel.me

CONTENTS

INTRODUCTION

Picture the scene ...

It's 1984 and a lonely, heartbroken child called Mel sits in her bedroom playing 'Bagsy That' with her younger sister and the Freemans catalogue. She is heartbroken because Shakin' Stevens is swanning off, doing duets with Bonnie Tyler and because 'Look In' magazine has no pictures of him this week to stick on her wall. It's all going wrong. If only she had the Ra-Ra skirt on page 985, and if only she were as cool as Denise Huxtable from 'The Cosby Show', then Shaky would marry her and everything would be okay.

The two sisters become bored of the catalogue game when they reach the kitchen appliance section and, instead, take to playing their illegal radio recording of the 'Top 40' on a TDK90 cassette. They write down the lyrics to Madonna's 'Borderline' and begin devising a dance routine that resembles rhythmic sign language. Mel then rushes downstairs after hearing the music from 'Hart Beat' blaring from the rented telly, and for half an hour, she sits mesmerised, taking everything in.

Well, 28 years later, here I am and I *did* take everything in. Tony Hart would be proud to know that, thanks to him, I am now an artist and designer, about to share with you my nostalgic look at the 1980s using a whole year's worth of '80s themed projects that you can make and do all by yourself. Because, way back in the days when dog poo was white and Raleigh choppers weren't just for the hipsters of East London, we didn't have an array of Internet-ready gadgets to occupy us like we do now. We had fashion wheels and painting-by-numbers. We had colouring-in and paper dolls. And we had time. Or, at least, we did before *The Littlest Hobo*, *Jim'll Fix It!* and *The Fall Guy* started!

This *1980s Bumper Activity Book* will provide you with a mixture of retro techniques along with modern-day projects with an '80s twist. Cool projects though, way better than the stuff they made on *Blue Peter*. So what are you waiting for? Switch off the telly, get your scissors out and enjoy!

At the bottom of each project start page is your essential soundtrack.

Borderline
Madonna

Why don't you make up your own dance routine to this one?

A Bordeline MADONNA

Here is your entire soundtrack.

A DATE/TIME NOISE REDUCTION ☐ ON ☐ OFF	**B** DATE/TIME NOISE REDUCTION ☐ ON ☐ OFF
'It Ain't What You Do' – Bananarama & Fun Boy3	'I Ran' – A Flock Of Seagulls
'Toy Soldiers' – Martika	'Hold On Tight' – ELO
'Theme From S Express' – S'Express	'Pass The Dutchie' – Musical Youth
'Dress You Up' – Madonna	'Smooth Operator' – SADE
'Fight For Your Right' – The Beastie Boys	'Club Tropicana' – WHAM!
'Relax' – Frankie Goes To Hollywood	'China In Your Hand' – T'Pau
'Don't Talk To Me About Love' – Altered Images	'19' – Paul Hardcastle
'Sonic Boom Boy' – Westworld	'I Melt With You' – Modern English
'When Love Breaks Down' – Prefab Sprout	'Wild In The Country' – Bow Wow Wow
'Sowing the Seeds Of Love' – Tears For Fears	'99 Red Balloons' – Nena
'Joe Le Taxi' – Vanessa Paradis	'Oh Yeah' – Yello
'You Drive Me Crazy' – Shakin' Stevens	'Mad About You' – Belinda Carlisle
'Black Coffee In Bed' – Squeeze	'Notorious' – Duran Duran

It's available as a playlist on SPOTIFY... '80s Bumper Book'

80s Bumper Book

SA 90

A Live It Up – Mental As Anything

A DATE/TIME NOISE REDUCTION ☐ ON ☐ OFF	**B** DATE/TIME NOISE REDUCTION ☐ ON ☐ OFF
'Wild Thing' – Tone Loc	'Together in Electric Dreams' – Human League
'Pretty In Pink' – The Psychedelic Furs	'Walk this Way' – RUN DMC & Aerosmith
'Perfect Circle' – REM	'Love Plus One' – Haircut 100
'Perfect Kiss' – New Order	'Rapture' – Blondie
'In the Air Tonight' – Phil Collins	'Thriller' – Michael Jackson
'Buffalo Stance' – Neneh Cherry	'Reward' – The Teardrop Explodes
'Let's Go Crazy' – Prince	'We Got the Beat' – The Go-Gos
'Opportunities' – The Pet Shop Boys	'The Riddle' – Nik Kershaw
'New Sensation' – INXS	'Here Comes Your Man' – The Pixies
'Electric Youth' – Debbie Gibson	'She Bop' – Cyndi Lauper
'What Difference Does It Make?' – The Smiths	'Walk Out to Winter' – Aztec Camera
'The Story Of the Blues' – The Mighty Wah!	'Always On My Mind' – Pet Shop Boys
'The Sun Always Shines on TV' – A-Ha	'Do They Know It's Christmas?' – Band Aid

SA 90

Go to www.spotify.com and sign up if you haven't already.
Then simply search for '80s Bumper Book' by Mellyelliott

COLOURING IN

Use your felt-tips to colour in some classic '80s toys.

Toy Soldiers
Martika

MAJOR T.M.
MORGAN

A B C D
D E F G
G A B C
C D E F

'POST-IT' WALL MURAL

This is such an easy and effective project.
The wall pictured is in my own kitchen, but it would be great in a kid's bedroom, study or downstairs loo (where visitors could leave you messages on the Post-it notes!).

To create this, I started by painting my wall in blackboard paint (we also use this particular wall to chalk notes, recipes and to play extreme pictionary after a few Babychams).

*Theme From
S Express*
S'Express

So, start by picking a wall. Now, obviously this looks most effective if the wall is painted black, although any dark colour such as navy or grey would work well. This is still a nice project to do on a white or cream wall though so don't feel excluded if decorating in black is a bit drastic for you (personally I find black dramatic and sophisticated in the home, and my taste in music probably informs you that I'm far from goth-like!).

Get yourself some brightly coloured Post-it notes ... making sure that you get the square ones. You will also need some double-sided sticky tape.

Using the grid guide provided, overleaf, start placing your Post-it notes to form the shapes, it's so easy, even a cat can do it!

Once you are happy with your positioning, one by one, remove each Post-it note, attach a bit of double-sided tape to the back before placing it back in position (if you don't do this, they tend to fall off after just a few hours).

I have kept my design simple, but feel free to add as many space invaders as you like!

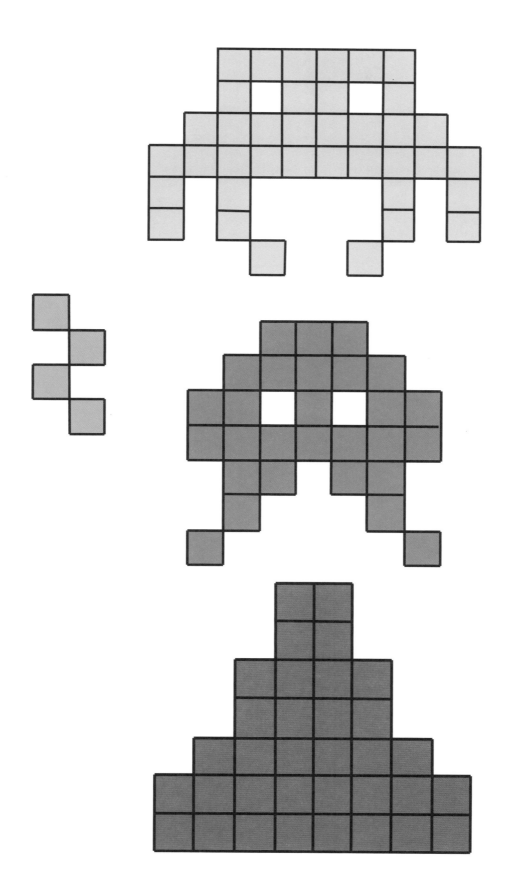

COLOURING IN

Use your felt-tips to colour in this '8Os classic, the Volkswagen Golf GTI.

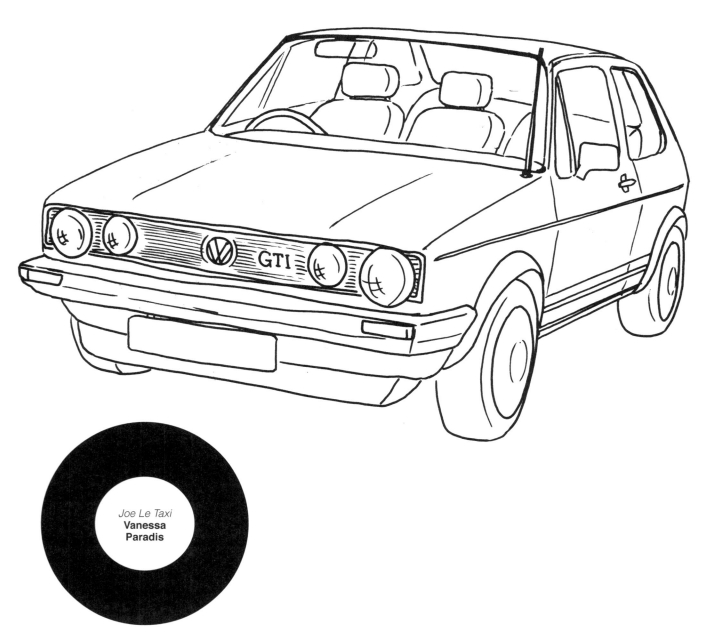

Joe Le Taxi
**Vanessa
Paradis**

MAGNUM P.I. PAPER DOLL

Thomas Magnum owned the best moustache known to womankind – followed closely by Nigel Mansell and Kevin Webster. He also had a Ferrari F308 GTS, a couple of dobermans, plenty of chest hair and a grumpy butler named Higgins. He ran around every Saturday afternoon (after I'd been to C&A with my mum), wearing skimpy shorts and open Hawaiian shirts, and he also solved crimes or something.

He lived in a massive house with a big fence but it didn't belong to him, it belonged to some guy who was on a long holiday. The Ferrari wasn't Magnum's either, or the dogs, or the butler. The only thing he owned was his moustache.

Magnum (who was so cool, they named an ice lolly after him) was played brilliantly by Tom Selleck, who went on to become a Monica-snogging eye doctor in *Friends*.

Fun Magnum Fact
Magnum was only set in Hawaii because *Hawaii-5-0* had just ended and the CBS network didn't want to close down it's production office there.

Using spray adhesive, stick the paper doll, including the stand, to a bit of card – an empty cereal packet will work perfectly. Then carefully cut around the doll figure using a craft knife or scissors. There's no need to stick the outfits onto card, just cut them out and then dress and undress Magnum at your pleasure!

Dress You Up
Madonna

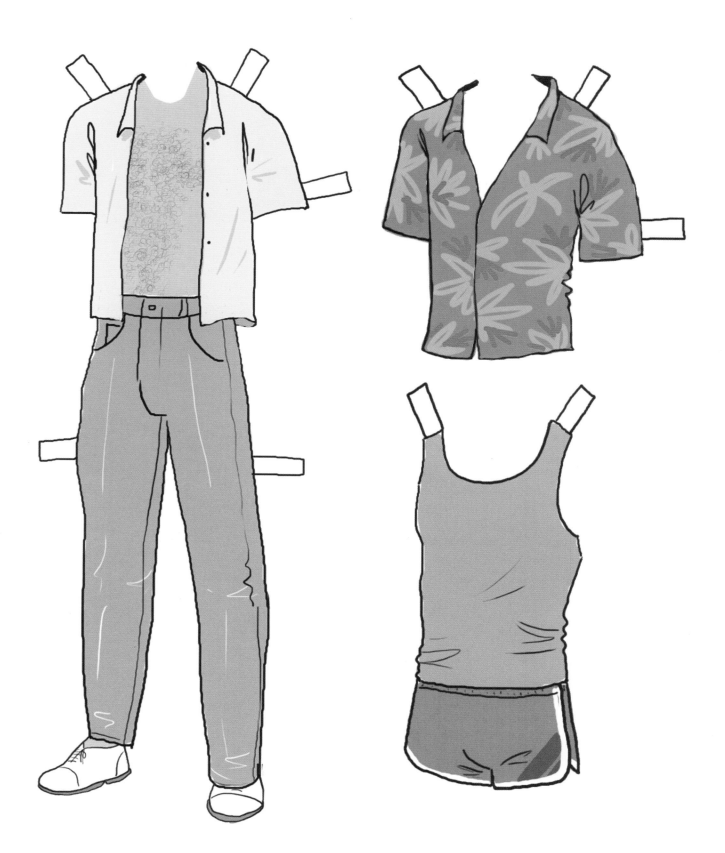

FANCY DRESS COSTUME

Need a couple's '80s fancy dress idea? Go as the song '99 Red Balloons' by Nena! Simply attach 50 and 49 red balloons to string, to make a balloon garland, then wrap around yours and your partner's bodies. Then get ready for people mistaking you for raspberries!

99 Red Balloons
Nena

3-D PAPER DELOREAN

The DeLorean DMC–12 was produced in Belfast and for a very, very limited time only (1981-1982).

John DeLorean was famously arrested in 1981 and was eventually released without charge. However, those events led to the bankruptcy of the DeLorean Motor Company. The DeLorean was, of course, the time machine in the *Back To The Future* movie trilogy. You could buy the car in any colour as long as it was *un*coloured. (The DeLorean came, unpainted, in polished stainless steel, except for three cars, which were plated in 24-carat gold and cost $85,000 each – which was a lot of money in the '80s!).

Even without it's gold plating, the DMC–12 was a very expensive car and probably had one of those fancy cassette players that turned your tape over for you. Remember them?

Sonic Boom Boy
Westworld

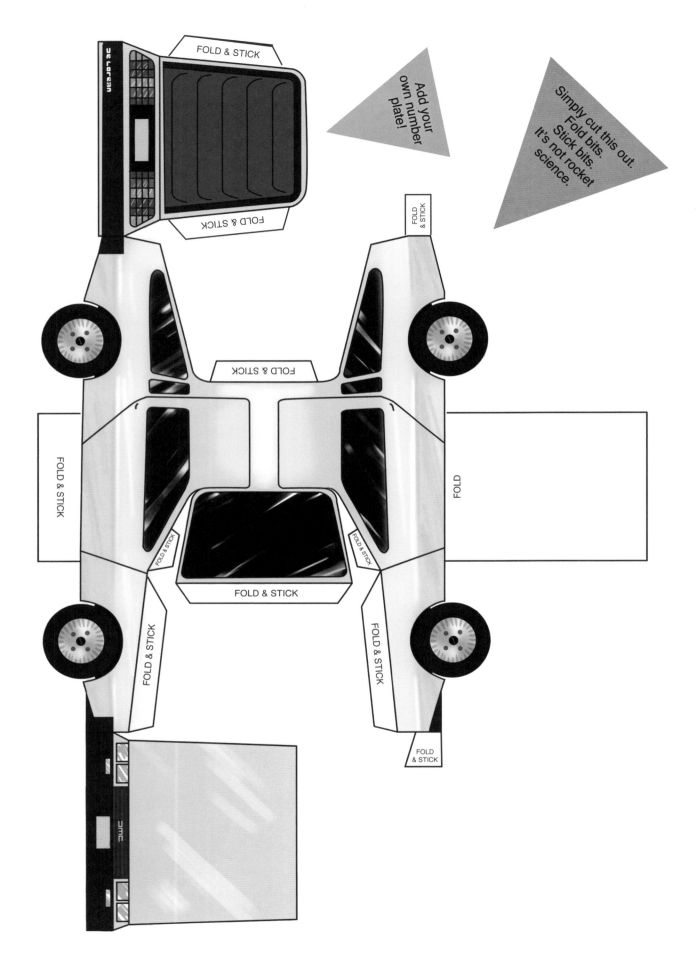

FOLD & STICK

FOLD & STICK

De Lorean

Add your
own number
plate!

Simply cut this out.
Fold bits.
Stick bits.
It's not rocket
science.

FOLD
& STICK

FOLD & STICK

FOLD & STICK

FOLD & STICK

FOLD

FOLD & STICK

FOLD & STICK

FOLD & STICK

FOLD & STICK

FOLD & STICK

FOLD
& STICK

DMC

DANIEL-SAN HEADBAND

Karate Kid was released in 1984, and was the story of Daniel (played by Ralph Macchio), a bullied teenager, who takes up karate. His wise teacher, Mr. Miyagi, shows him how to clean cars, paint fences, catch flies and stand on one leg for very long periods of time while audiences everywhere yelled 'Just show him how to flipping kick people!'.

Daniel's love intesrest was Ali (played by Elizabeth Shue) who, to me, looked a bit old and big for little Ralph. She went on to snog Tom Cruise in *Cocktail*.

You'll be pleased to know that Daniel did get quite good at karate in the end.

You don't need to be into martial arts to wear this headband, simply wear it down the pub and become a trendsetter!

To begin, you'll need some white fabric (the bottom of an old T-Shirt will do!). Ensure that your piece is long enough to tie around your forehead. It is completely up to you and your ability as to whether you paint or stencil.

If you decide to stencil, simply cut out the pattern from the template and follow the instructions as per week 11.

If you want to paint your design on, use Dylon Fabric Paint. (In the film, the design is a navy blue colour, but if you use black, you can use the same fabric paint for the project demonstrated in week 12).

Use a good quality artist's brush (around a size 9) and very lightly draw the design in pencil, onto your fabric before painting.

When Love Breaks Down
Prefab Sprout

21

Fold in the sides and
secure with iron-on
adhesive

MICRO CROSS-STITCH

Cross-stitch doesn't have to be all *Little House On The Prairie* and 'Home Sweet Home' you know! 8-BIT technology used in '80s computer gaming lends itself brilliantly to cross-stitch patterns.

Here is a little taster in the form of Bob Carolgees look-a-like, and Italian plumber supremo, Super Mario! This is a pattern I devised myself but feel free to come up with your own too!

Firstly, you will need a piece of 14-count cross-stitch canvas 14.85cm x 10.5cm, that way you can put him into a postcard-sized frame or on a greetings card.

You will also need the following Anchor colours
(or just use what you can get hold of):

Blue: 134
Red: 46
Yellow: 291
Brown: 351
Flesh: 4146
Black

Sowing The Seeds Of Love
Tears For Fears

To start off your cross-stitch, bring your needle up through the fabric, leaving a short piece of thread at the back ...

Tuck this into your first few stitches so that it stays in place.

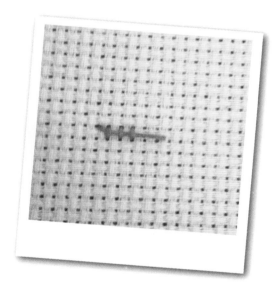

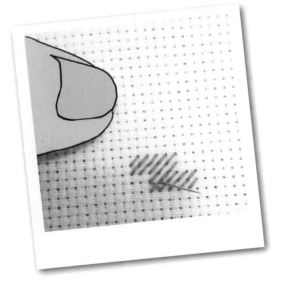

Do your diagonals before reversing and adding your crosses.

To start off a new colour, run it through the back of the existing stitches.

To finish a colour, run your thread underneath a few stitches at the back to secure it.

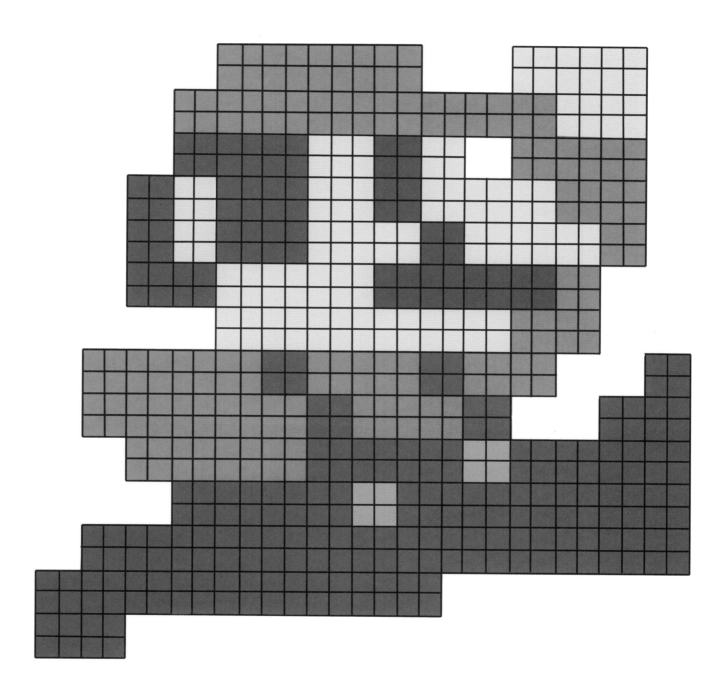

COLOURING IN

Use your felt-tips to colour in Arnold from *Diff'rent Strokes*.

Whatchoo Talkin' 'Bout Willis?

Smooth Operator
Sade

MEGA YUMMY PAC-MAN CAKE

YOU WILL NEED

FOR THE CAKE
175g butter or margarine (softened)
175g caster sugar
3 eggs, lightly beaten with 1–2tsp vanilla essence
175g self-raising flour (sifted)

FOR THE CENTRE
Strawberry or raspberry jam
125g unsalted butter (softened)
250g icing sugar

FOR THE DECORATION
1 block of yellow sugar paste
1 block of black sugar paste

FOR THE EATING
A mouth and a belly

FOR THE CLEANING UP
A friend

Fight For Your Right
The Beastie Boys

PREHEAT YOUR OVEN TO 180°...

LINE A 21cm CAKE TIN WITH GREASEPROOF PAPER...

CREAM THE BUTTER AND SUGAR TOGETHER IN A MIXING BOWL UNTIL LIGHT AND FLUFFY. GENTLY ADD THE EGG AND VANILLA MIXTURE, THEN BEAT UNTIL COMBINED. GRADUALLY FOLD IN THE FLOUR AND COMBINE THE INGREDIENTS BUT DO NOT OVER-WORK THE MIXTURE!!

POUR THE MIXTURE INTO THE TIN AND FLATTEN WITH A WET KNIFE...

PUT IN THE CENTRE OF THE OVEN FOR 30 MINUTES AND THEN... TA-DAAAH!!!

MEANWHILE...

BEAT THE BUTTER AND ICING SUGAR TOGETHER UNTIL LIGHT AND FLUFFY

ONCE THE CAKE HAS COOLED, CUT IT IN HALF. SPREAD SOME OF THE BUTTER-CREAM EVENLY ON THE BOTTOM HALF OF THE CAKE (YOU WILL NEED ABOUT ONE THIRD OF THE MIXTURE FOR A LATER STAGE) AND THE JAM ON THE TOP HALF.

PLACE THE TOP HALF BACK ONTO THE CAKE TO MAKE THE SANDWICH

CUT AN EIGHTH OUT OF THE CAKE TO MAKE...

THE MOUTH OF PAC-MAN!

PUT A SMALL AMOUNT OF BUTTER-CREAM ON YOUR SURFACE TO PREVENT SLIPPING, THEN...

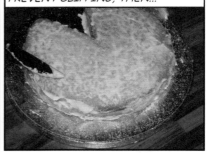

SPREAD A THIN LAYER OF BUTTER-CREAM OVER THE TOP AND SIDES OF THE CAKE. SAVE A TINY AMOUNT OF ANY LEFT OVER BUTTER-CREAM TO APPLY THE EYE AT A LATER STAGE.

ROLL OUT YOUR YELLOW SUGAR PASTE TO ROUGHLY 3mm IN THICKNESS, ENSURING THAT THE AREA ROLLED WILL COVER THE ENTIRE CAKE.

WOAH!!

TAKE A SHARP KNIFE AND CUT AROUND THE EDGE OF THE SUGAR PASTE

GENTLY PEEL THIS OFF THE BASE AND SAVE A SMALL AMOUNT FOR LATER

AND THEN...

CLEAN UP AROUND THE MOUTH SO THAT THE INSIDE OF THE CAKE IS SHOWING.

MEGA!!!

ROLL OUT YOUR BLACK SUGAR PASTE AND CUT TWO STRIPS OUT, THAT ARE ROUGHLY THE SAME HEIGHT AS YOUR CAKE...

USING A SMALL ROUND CUTTER, CUT OUT A CIRCLE FROM THE BLACK SUGAR PASTE (THIS WILL FORM THE EYE). TAKE THE CIRCLE AND SLICE A SMALL TRIANGLE OUT OF ONE EDGE.

AND LOOK!! YOUR VERY OWN PAC-MAN CAKE!!!

SCOFF IT! YUM YUM!!

Delicious!!

SLOGAN T-SHIRT

In 1983, fashion designer Katharine Hamnett designed the first, over-sized, anti-establishment slogan T-Shirt, and they have been a phenomenon ever since. Slogans such as 'CHOOSE LIFE' and 'STAY ALIVE IN 85' made political comment on global events such as the AIDS virus and the Falklands War. The T-Shirts were worn proudly by leading pop stars such as George Michael and Roger Taylor before being copied by Frankie Goes To Hollywood with 'FRANKIE SAYS RELAX'.

Hamnett's intention with the slogan T-Shirt concept was to give people a voice and to get important messages across ... so it is with this in mind, that I give you my T-Shirt slogan ...

Relax
Frankie Goes To Hollywood

Firstly, cut out the pages from this book, photocopy them, or download the T-Shirt artwork from www.80sbumperbook.com. Then, with a craft knife, **very carefully**, cut out each letter from the two sheets. Making sure to save any letters with white middles (B, D, O, A, P and R).

Carefully, with a steady hand, cut out the white centres of these letters, and save.
Insert something into your T-Shirt (I used the back of an A3 sketchpad) to keep the surface nice and smooth, but also to stop the paint from seeping through onto the back of your T-Shirt. Then spray the back of your stencil and the back of your white letter centres, with spray adhesive.

Stick this onto the front of your T-Shirt, pressing down firmly onto all the edges. Place the letter centres into position also and press down. Cover up the remainder of the T-Shirt, so as not to accidentally spray that too. Use the spray paint lightly and go back over any areas that don't get covered. **Do this as quickly as possible**. Leave for a minute before carefully peeling back your stencil, and then use your craft knife to lift off the white centres. Now RELAX! Your T-Shirt needs to rest for a good hour or so before wearing and please allow a few days before washing at 30°.

NOBODY

BODY

PUTS BABY

BABY

IN THE CORNER

PRINT YOUR SKINNY TIE

TO MAKE A SPARKLING PIANO PRINT TIE...

ATTACH A STRIP OF FOAM OR SPONGE TO A MATCHBOX.

USING A PAINTBRUSH, PAINT THE FOAM WITH BLACK FABRIC PAINT.

THEN PRINT ONE BLACK KEY ALONE, FOLLOWED BY TWO, CLOSE TOGETHER, AND SO ON AND SO ON.

TO ADD GLITTER, PAINT OVER THE BLACK KEYS WITH FABRIC GLUE...

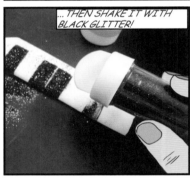

...THEN SHAKE IT WITH BLACK GLITTER!

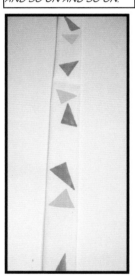

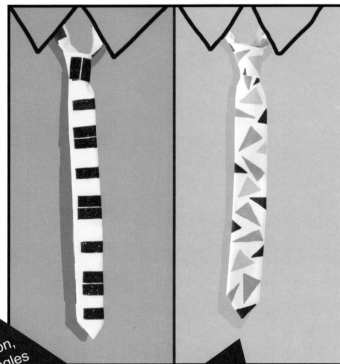

Let's Go Crazy
Prince & The Revolution

For a more colourful option, use foam triangles and print randomly using bright colours!

This pattern looks ace on a skirt!

EASY GUITAR – SHAKY

Shakin' Stevens drove me crazy from a very tender age. I was a 'gig virgin' before going to see him in Blackpool with my big cousin Alison (I screamed for hours when she presented me with my ticket!). After Shaky had sung and danced his heart out, I bought myself a white satin fringed cushion with his perfect pouty face emblazoned upon it. This cushion was my pride and joy and it sat majestically upon my Pierrot the Clown continental quilt cover.

I wasn't the only Shaky fan though, he was the UK's biggest selling singles artist of the 1980s, with a whopping 33 Top 40 singles, and in 1985 he became the first artist to appear on *Top Of The Pops* 50 times!

The Shaky song we are going to learn is 'You Drive Me Crazy', written by Ronnie Harwood. It was featured on the 1981 album entitled *Shaky.* This is my favourite album because he wears a lovely pink jacket and points wantonly at me from the cover.

This is such a simple and beautiful song, easy to learn and sounds wonderful played on an accoustic guitar. Have fun!

You Drive Me Crazy **Shakin' Stevens**

```
D                                    G      A
You know baby when you're in my arms
D               G          A
I can feel your loving, magic charms
            D       G  A
You drive me crazy
            D        G  A
You drive me crazy
D                                      G        A
And when I'm looking in those big blue eyes
D                     G     A
I start flowing down in paradise
            D       G  A
You drive me crazy
G                              A
Heaven must have sent you down
G                            A
Down for you to give me a thrill
G
Everytime you touch me, everytime you hold me
A
My heart starts beating like a train on a track
D                       G       A
I love you baby and it's plain to see
D                       G        A
I love you honey it was meant to be
            D      G  A
You drive me crazy
            D      G  A
You drive me crazy
```

G   A

Heaven must have sent you down

G   A

Down for you to give me a thrill

G

Everytime you touch me, everytime you hold me

A

My heart starts beating like a train on a track

D   G   A

I love you baby and it's plain to see

D   G   A

I love you honey it was meant to be

                     D   G   A

You drive me crazy

                     D   G   A

You drive me crazy

                     D   G   A

You drive me crazy

                     D   G   A

You drive me crazy

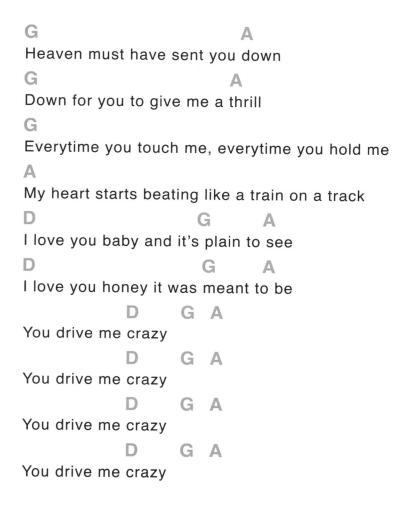

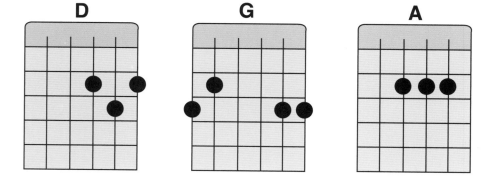

'You Drive Me Crazy' written by Ronnie Harwood. Chords arranged by Mel.

COLOURING IN

Use your felt-tips to colour in this iconic scene from *Risky Business*.

In The Air Tonight
Phil Collins

'80s POP COLLAGE

Collage is such an easy and satisfying thing to do. Simply get yourself some scissors or a craft knife, use spray adhesive or stick glue, embrace your inner child and get to work. The theme for this project is simply 'Pop Culture', so, get researching on the Internet and print out any images that you wish to include. Look at the decade's toys, the films, the TV shows, the music, the fashion, the politics and even the food!

Then, *without* using your glue, arrange them upon a white piece of paper until you reach a composition that you like the look of. There are no rules here, simply use your instincts and have fun with it.

When you are happy with your creation, begin sticking the pieces into place, starting at the bottom so that any overlapping pieces are stuck down last.

For a bit of experimentation, try printing your images onto different coloured paper, graph paper or even foolscap. Try it!

I Ran (So Far Away) **A Flock Of Seagulls**

You'll be needing your collage for week 33 but you can always use this if you're not happy with your own!

LEGO PROTEST PICTURE

In 1986, the cast of *Grange Hill* bravely held their hands over their headphones and sang about how drugs were bad. These kids had a dance routine and were not to be messed with. Using the language of pop, they told us that you could choose between ending up with a semi-decent part in *London's Burning*, or as a contestant on *Celebrity Scissorhands*, with three simple words ...

Pass The Dutchie
Musical Youth

First, you will need to go out and buy a 38 x 38cm flat Lego board (the stuff you stick your Lego onto, it usually comes in grey or green).

From the top of your board, count four bumps down and seven across. This is where you will start building your words.

Use the letter templates over the page.

Leave a gap of three bumps in between each letter and leave a gap of five bumps in between each line.

Shadow your letters with different colours in single bump strips.

Add a two-bump border around the word 'SAY'.

Once you have completed your Lego text, you may want to frame it.

Buy a deep, 50 x 50cm frame and and use a hot glue-gun to attach your Lego board to the front of the card mount (which will probably come with the frame).

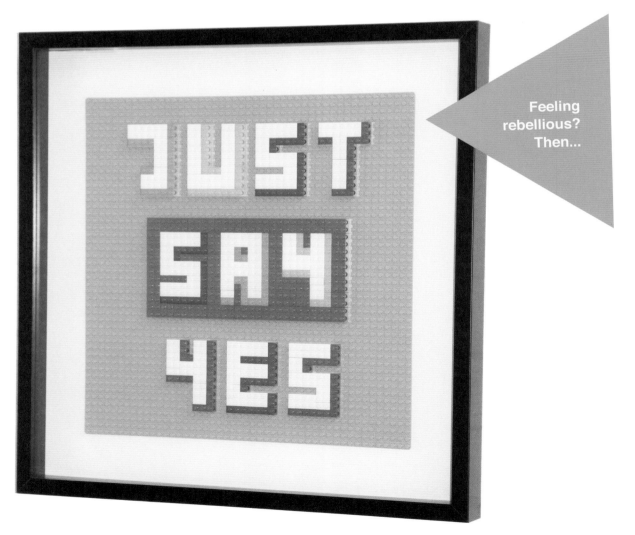

Feeling rebellious? Then...

Here are your letter templates!

Charles & Di and Andrew & Fergie both had official commemorative plates when they married in the '80s. However, Madonna and Sean Penn didn't. So let's try and put that right ...

COMMEMORATIVE PLATE

MADONNA

16ᵗʰ August 1985

SEAN

China In Your Hand
T'Pau

1

For this project, we are using some special stuff called 'Lazertran' and it is made for laser printers and photocopiers. However, if you have an inkjet printer, there are other types of paper you can use to transfer images onto ceramics.

2

Print the images onto your ceramic transfer paper (Lazertran, or otherwise). Your image must be printed onto the slightly shiny side of the paper. You can download the images from www.80sbumperbook.com

3

Cut out the image components separately like so ...

4

Then starting with the central image, soak each part in a bowl of water. Leave to soak for around 30 seconds, or until the backing starts to become loose. Place the image onto your plate and then gently slide the paper from beneath the thin film. Smooth down any creases or bubbles. Continue with all the small images around the plate's rim and leave to dry.

Play with scale & different objects!

MADONNA

16TH August 1985

SEAN

EIGHTIFY YOUR SHADES

I was walking on sunshine the day I got my star and stripes Rayban-shaped shades from Chelsea Girl. Just like Timmy Mallet, I looked the business ... and now you can too!

Cut this template out of foam, sponge, glittery card, or just use the paper in this book! Stick to the front of your existing sunglasses and then go bonkers and do the 'Agadoo' or something.

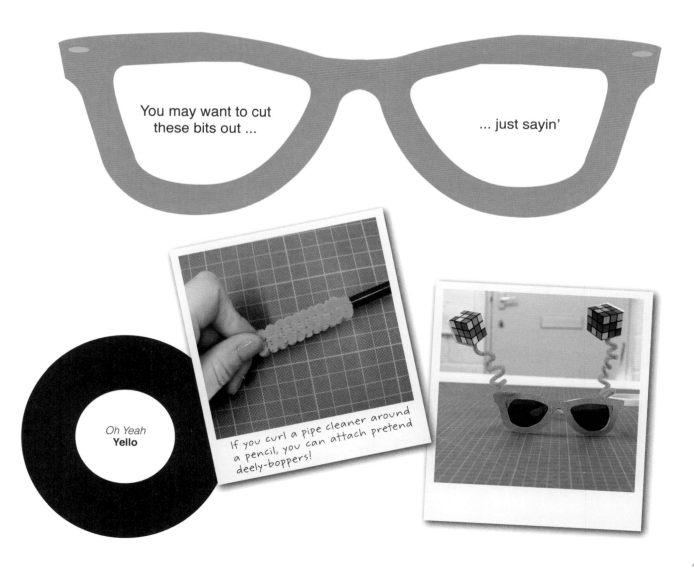

You may want to cut these bits out ...

... just sayin'

Oh Yeah
Yello

If you curl a pipe cleaner around a pencil, you can attach pretend deely-boppers!

Because Timmy Mallet is the influence behind this project, I think it's only fair to encourage you to play *the* best game of the '80s (except for *Blockbusters*, of course) MALLET'S MALLET!

1. Take two nervous people and sit them on chairs facing each other.

2. Get yourself a sponge mallet, an inflatable hammer, cushion or small tea tray (basically something to hit the nervous people over the head with but without hurting or killing them).

3. Then say this really quickly:

'Mallet's Mallet is a word association game, where you musn't pause, hesitate, repeat a word, or say a word I don't like...otherwise you get a bash on the head like this... (*bash the nervous people on the head*) **or like this...the one with the most bruises loses...look at each other and go Bleugh! Look at everyone at home and go Bleugh! Everyone at home look at them and go Bleugh!'**

4. Start them off with a word picked at random, or from a newspaper, magazine or even this book. Your word could be BOOK!

5. The first nervous person could say PAGE, the other person could say PAPER, then PULP, then JARVIS, then COCKER, then SPANIEL, then DOG and I'm sure you get the picture.

6. Play it after the next project ... and maybe after a few Cinzanos too!

PAINTING·BY·NUMBERS

Blue = B

Dark Brown = DB

Grey = G

Pink = P

Light Flesh = F1

Medium Flesh = F2

Dark Flesh = F3

Black = BL

White = Left Blank

I remember doing a 'Painting-by-Numbers' as a kid (when I became bored waiting for Shakin' Stevens to release another album). I think it was a stallion running through the sea and I wouldn't wish the finished article on my worst enemy (who at the time was Grotbags). I hope that you will get more enjoyment out of this project, and be proud to display your finished painting of '80s anti-hero, **Ferris Bueller**.

19
Paul Hardcastle

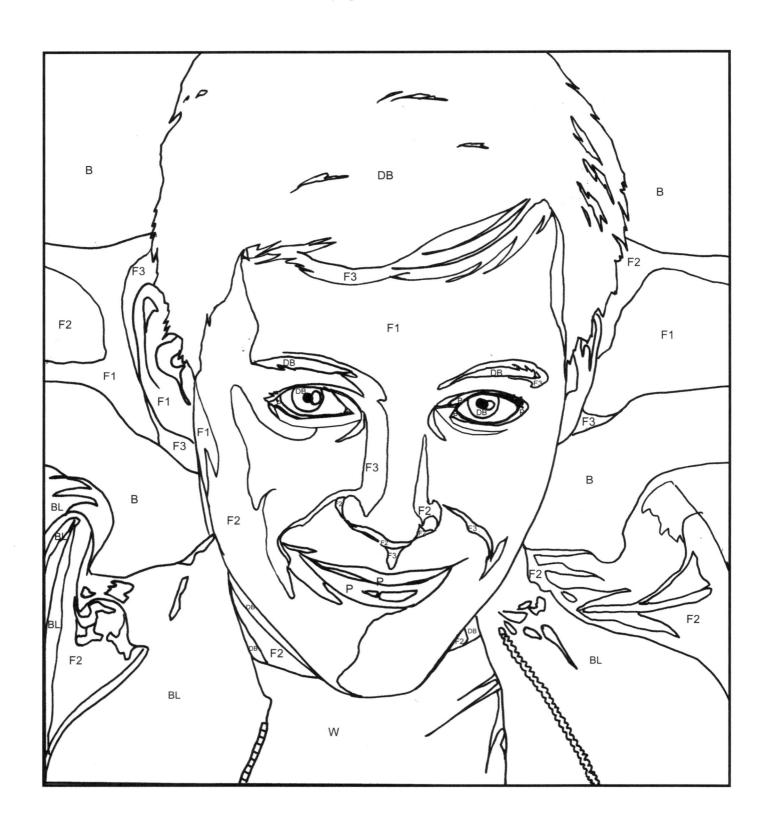

week 20

BAND T-SHIRTS

Siobhan &
Keren &
Sara.

Matt &
Luke &
Craig.

Pretty In Pink
**The
Psychedellic
Furs**

Follow the instructions as detailed
in Week 11 and use the templates
I have provided. Or, if you want,
make up your own!

Matt & Luke & Craig.

Stock & Aitken & Waterman.

Siobhan &
Keren &
Sara.

'PONG' DUVET COVER

I remember getting my first ever 'continental quilt' and my mum putting a Pierrot the Clown cover on it. Thinking back, it wasn't cool. This 'Pong' duvet is though! Before the likes of *Grand Theft Auto*, we had two white sticks and a square ball as computer virtual entertainment ... and it was great!

Black Coffee In Bed
Squeeze

Recreate this 'Pong' duvet cover using a very simple appliqué technique!

You will need...

A black (or dark-coloured) double duvet cover and two pillow cases, some white cotton fabric, some iron-on adhesive, and some white cotton thread.

Then...

1

Cut out your pieces of fabric using the guides provided here.

2

Cut the same shape from the iron-on adhesive.

3

Peel the backing from the iron-on adhesive and iron onto the fabric patch.

4

Iron this onto your duvet cover.

5

Hand-stitch around the edges, using the white thread.

6

Have the coolest bedroom in all the land!
Swap pillow cases depending on who is 'winning' in life!

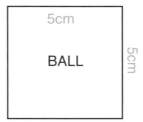

5cm

BALL

5cm

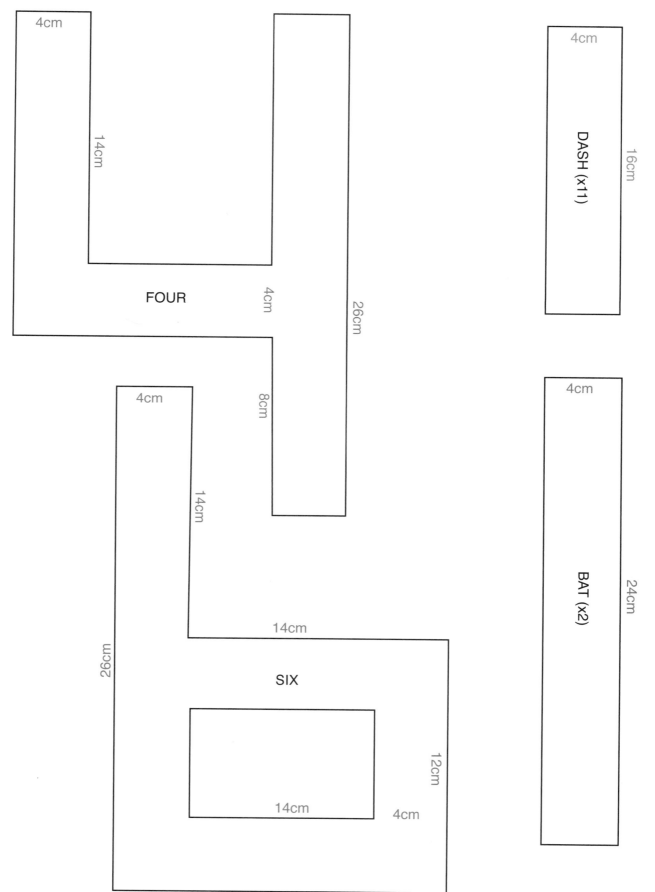

FOUR

4cm

14cm

4cm

26cm

8cm

4cm

14cm

26cm

SIX

14cm

14cm

12cm

4cm

DASH (x11)

4cm

16cm

BAT (x2)

4cm

24cm

week
22

TEMPORARY TATTOOS

See Week 32 for detailed instructions

MADONNA WALL STENCIL

Madonna is undoubtedly one of the most influencal pop artists of the '80s ... in fact, the whole of time! Celebrate her brilliance by channelling your inner graffiti artist and stencilling your walls!

Get a craft knife, and a cutting mat.

Carefully, cut out all the black from the image.

On the reverse, spray lightly with adhesive.

Press onto your wall and use newsprint to mask the rest of the wall.

Use spray paint, then peel off the stencil.

Mad About You
Belinda Carlisle

DRAW LIKE AN ETCH A SKETCH

Recreate the fun you had with this '80s classic.

DRAW LIKE AN *Etch A Sketch* ! IT'S REALLY HARD!

RULES: Use a pencil, but no lifting it off the page; only go vertical and diagonal. NO CHEATING!

IDEAS OF THINGS TO DRAW: a ghetto-blaster, an ice lolly, a baseball cap, a Ford Capri, an extra terrestrial.

Perfect Circle **REM**

DRAW LIKE AN *Etch A Sketch* ! IT'S REALLY HARD!

DRAW LIKE AN *Etch A Sketch* ! IT'S REALLY HARD!

week 25

LAMBORGHINI WALL STENCIL

I was a bit of a tom-boy as a child. I remember being about nine or ten and it being a 'non uniform day' at school. All the other girls wore their favourite Ra-Ra skirts, pretty socks and make-up ...

... I wore motorcycling leathers and a full-face helmet! In July!

This was one of my favourite cars. The Lamborghini Countach.

The Perfect Kiss
New Order

MAKE A SKINNY TIE

By the time you have finished this book, you will be an expert tie maker and will no longer be stuck for gift ideas for all those men who are hard to please. This is a difficult project, but it is a great skill to have!

Cut the following pieces out of your chosen fabric. You need to cut on the bias (this means that the grain of your fabric must be diagonal, rather than vertical/horizontal).

Note In week 12, I have shown you a fun way to decorate a skinny tie, so you may want to make this in a plain white fabric.

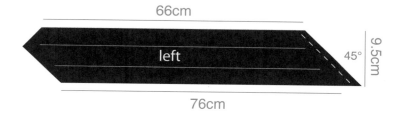

66cm

left

45° 9.5cm

76cm

40cm

middle

45° 9.5cm

22cm

Buffalo Stance **Neneh Cherry**

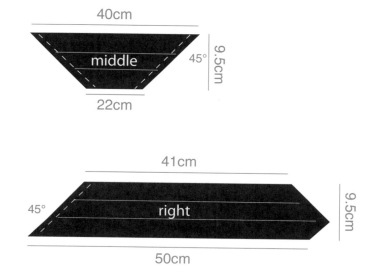

41cm

45° right 9.5cm

50cm

Sew the three pieces together along
the diagonal end of the middle piece.

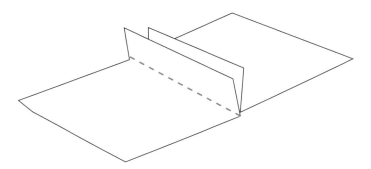

Iron the seams out flat ...

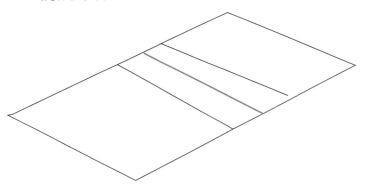

... so that you have something like this.

3

Take one long piece of iron-on interfacing
(3cm wide) and run down the middle
of your tie length.

Iron on!

4

Cute two pieces of your fabric,
this shape and size. These are
your facing pieces.

IMPORTANT!

Turn your tie length over, so you are
working on the posh front bit!

5

Sew the facing pieces to
each end of the tie length ...

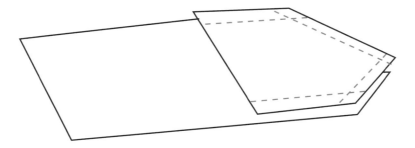

... then cut off the pointy bit!

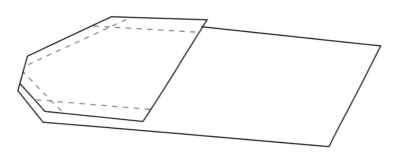

Turn these little pockets inside-out and then
iron them flat so that you have this:

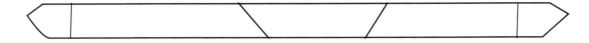

Fold in one edge. Fold in the other edge over it and tuck under.
Hand-stitch along the back length of your tie.

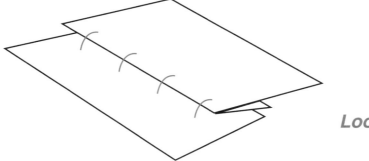

Look spiffing!

week 27

HARD RECORDER – THE FALL GUY

C C C C   C C C C   D C D   D   D C   EG
Well I'm not the kind to kiss and tell, but I've been seen with Farrah
G AA   A   A   AGGG G   C CD A G
I'm never seen with anything less than a nine, so fine
G A A A A A AG A   A   A AGGC   E
I've been on fire with Sally Field, gone fast with a girl named Bo
C D   D   D   D D c c   B A G
But somehow they just don't end up as mine

C C D   DDDD E E D C C   E C
It's a death defyin' life I lead, I take my chances
GA A A A A A G A G G   E D
I die for a livin' in the movies and TV
C   C D D   D D EE D D   C   C C E   C
But the hardest thing I ever do is watch my leading ladies
C   D   D D   D D D D c c   B A G
Kiss some other guy while I'm bandaging my knee

E G   A   A G A G A c c d   e   e   e   d   c
I might fall from a tall building, I might roll a brand new car
A   c   A c A G   C   C E   F E E D C
'Cause I'm the unknown stuntman that makes Redford such a star

D C C C   C   C C D   C D D   D C E G
I never spent much time in school but I taught ladies plenty
G A A A A A G G C D   A G
It's true I hire my body out for pay, hey hey

G   A G A   A G A G A   A   A G G C E
I've gotten burned over Cheryl Tiegs, blown up for Raquel Welch
C C   C D D D D c c BA G   A G
But when I end up in the hay it's only hay, hey hey

E G   A A   A G A   c   d e e   e   d c
I might jump an open drawbridge, or Tarzan from a vine
A   C A C A   G   C C E   F   E E D C
'Cause I'm the unknown stuntman, that makes Eastwood look so fine.

'The Unkown Stuntman'
by Glen Larson, Gail Jensen & David Somerville
Notes arranged by Mel.

Too hard? Use a kazoo!

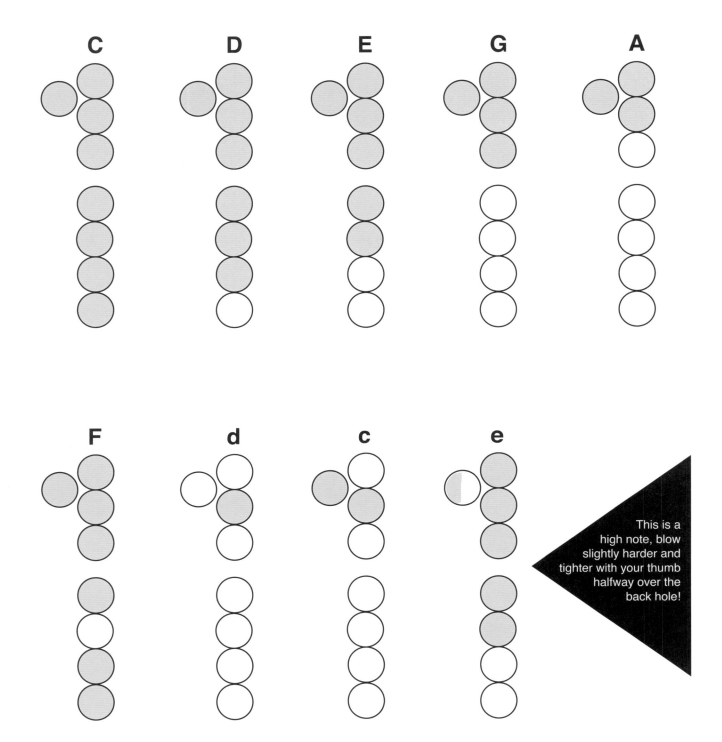

This is a high note, blow slightly harder and tighter with your thumb halfway over the back hole!

WHAM!
GLOVE PUPPETS

Club
Tropicana
Wham!

Wham! had suntans and wore skimpy shorts like no one else dared. They were made up of George Michael and Andrew Ridgeley and, to me, they epitomise '80s pop culture.

They sang cheerful songs in the '80s that made us happy (and they sang *the* best Christmas song ever ... that made us sad).

Make your home a happier place with these brilliantly simple Wham! glove puppets!

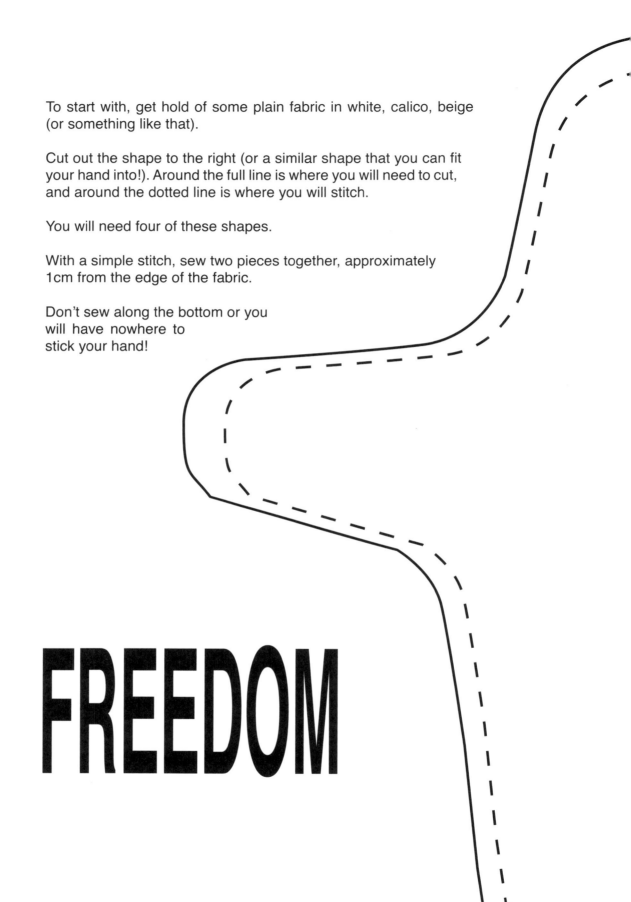

To start with, get hold of some plain fabric in white, calico, beige (or something like that).

Cut out the shape to the right (or a similar shape that you can fit your hand into!). Around the full line is where you will need to cut, and around the dotted line is where you will stitch.

You will need four of these shapes.

With a simple stitch, sew two pieces together, approximately 1cm from the edge of the fabric.

Don't sew along the bottom or you will have nowhere to stick your hand!

FREEDOM

Once you have sewn both your puppet shapes, you will need to Whamify them!

To do this, we are going to use the same transfer paper and technique that we will also use for Week 33.

Simply photocopy (or download from www.80sbumperbook.com) the heads and T-Shirt slogans, onto your fabric transfer paper, and then iron on.

Then have hours of fun singing and playing – but don't let anyone see you though!

CHOOSE LIFE

STOP·MOTION ANIMATION

With all the latest technology these days, stop-motion animation has never been easier to do yourself at home. You'll be amazed at what you can achieve with the simplest of materials.

I used my iPad and the *StopMotion* app pretty much does the job for you!

If you use an iPhone, the *StopMotionRecorder* app is incredibly easy to use.

Please give this ago, you'll be stop-motion animating anything (and everything) from then on!

To achieve the 'Pong Animation' (which you can see on www.80sbumperbook.com), I very simply used a sheet of black card and some bits of white paper. Move the bits of paper, by a small amount each time and take your photograph using your chosen device and app. Then the app will add your images together so that you can play them back. You can send this straight to YouTube or to iMovies, where you can edit it further, add credits and sound effects.

Together In Electric Dreams **The Human League**

ALEXIS CARRINGTON PAPER DOLL

Alexis Carrington was a TV character in the show *Dynasty* and she would have fisticuffs with anyone who so much as looked at her in the wrong way. She started off by fighting Krystle, but then, in season nine, her attentions moved onto Sable Colby. I'm not sure if there was an ultimate winner in all this fighting, but I hope it was Alexis. She looked better in fur than the animal it came from and her desk was made from not one, but two elephants. She was played brilliantly by the legendary Joan Collins and was the most glamorous woman on TV in the '80s (until, that is, Paula Hamilton left her husband in the VW Golf advert).

Fun Alexis Fact
Joan Collins was only eleven years older than the actor who played her son (Gordon Thompson).

Using spray adhesive, stick the paper doll, including the semi-circle stand, to a bit of card, an empty cereal packet will do. Then carefully cut around the doll figure using a craft knife or scissors. There's no need to stick the outfits onto card, just cut them out and then dress Alexis in whatever takes your fancy.

Notorious
Duran Duran

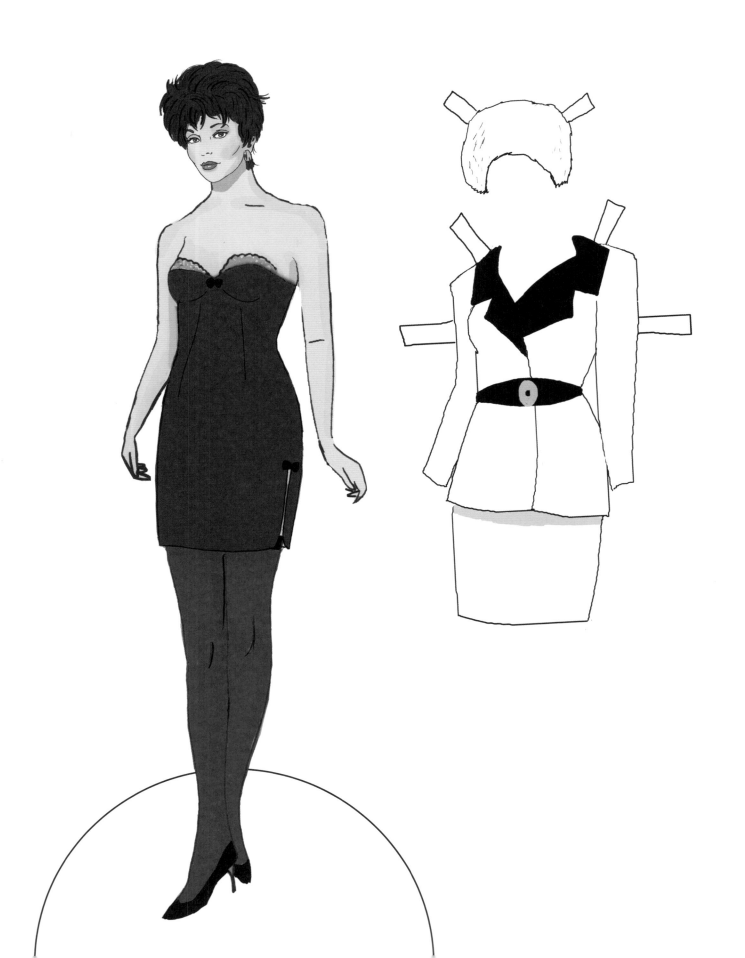

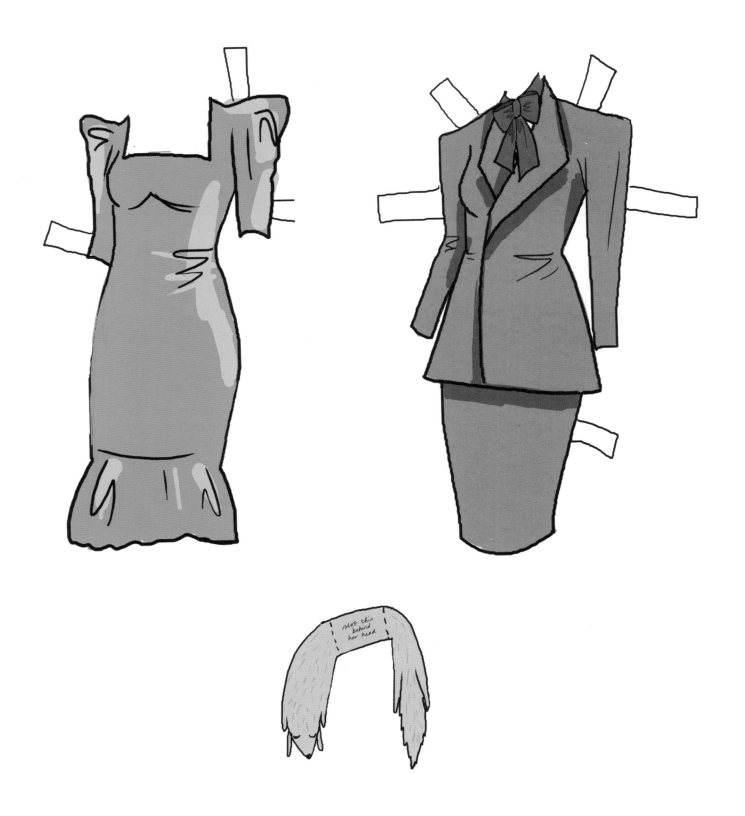

slot this
behind
her head

COLOURING IN

WALK THIS WAY

Walk this
Way
RUN DMC
feat
Aerosmith

MORE TEMPORARY TATTOOS

Want to be the envy of all your friends and become the coolest member of your gang?

Well now you can be, with the help of a few strategically placed temporary tattoos.

First you will need to get some tattoo transfer paper to go with your printer or photocopier. You will need to know if it is laser or inkjet as the transfer papers for each type differ. To do all the tattoo designs in this book, you will need four sheets (and they usually come in packs of five).

1. Scan the tattoo designs from this book and then print from your computer onto your transfer paper. Do not worry that the images are back to front, they are supposed to be.
2. Photocopy them straight onto the shiny side of your transfer paper.
3. Download the designs from 80sbumperbook. com and then print onto the transfer paper. Once printed, leave for at least one hour, before laying the shiny, adhesive sheet over the top and then rubbing out any air bubbles. When this is done, you can cut around your images with scissors or a craft knife and you're ready to go!

1. Peel off the clear, shiny backing paper.
2. Place the sticky decal face down on your skin, wherever you choose on your body, and press down firmly.
3. Sprinkle or use a paint brush to add water to the white backing until it becomes saturated.
4. After 20–30 seconds, the paper will easily slip off the tattoo.
5. Dab off excess water and leave to dry ...

LOOK INSTANTLY COOLER!

Wild Thing
Tone -Loc

RELAX

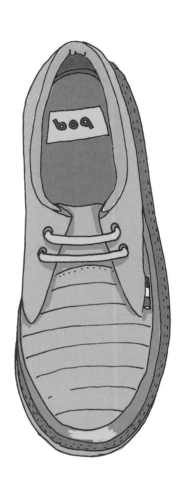

Nobody Puts Baby In The Corner!

stock
aitken &
waterman

week
33

TOTE BAG TRANSFER

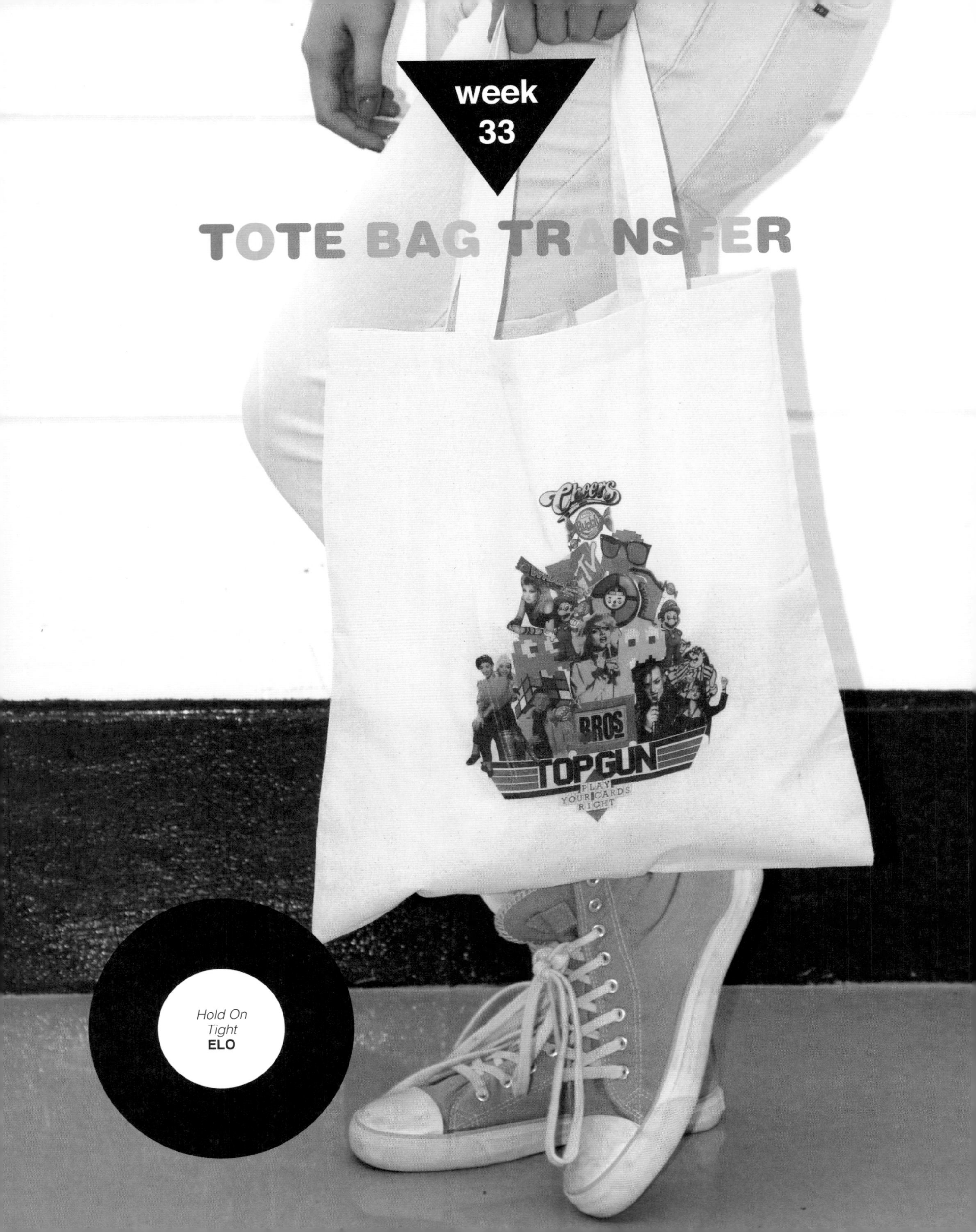

Hold On Tight
ELO

Print your design onto heat transfer paper. Remember to reverse your image.

Carefully, using scissors or a craft knife, cut out your design. Leave about a 3mm border.

Your image should look something like this.

Iron your design onto your canvas bag.

Leave to cool for five minutes, then carefully peel off the backing paper off the transfer paper.

And there you have it! You can carry stuff about, all over the place!

With lots of pressure place the iron on each part for 1–20 seconds. Do not use the steam setting!

Why not also try your collage design on a T-Shirt?

I used scissors to crop the bottom and widen the neck.

3-D PAPER YUPPIE TOY

In 1987, Nokia released the Cityman 3120. It was 20cm in height and weighed the same as Drew Barrymore from *E.T.* It was carried around by City boys and they would shout 'Okay yah!' into it at every given opportunity and discuss all the money they were making, whilst drinking fizzy water that wasn't even from a soda-stream!
They had PAID FOR IT!
They had BOUGHT WATER!
Even Tony Hart wasn't *that* posh.

These 'Yuppie types' were so fascinating to a family from Barnsley, like mine, that whenever we would go to London we'd just stare at them. I would point and say things like, 'Look dad! That one has his shirt collar up and is reading from a tiny ring-binder!'.

Well, now *you* can be a yuppie too!

On the following page is a cut-out 3-D model of the Nokia 3120, along with instructions on how to make a life-sized one. So, get your craft knife out, and after a bit of cutting and folding, you'll be well on your way to your first Porsche 911, okay yah?

Opportunities
Pet Shop Boys

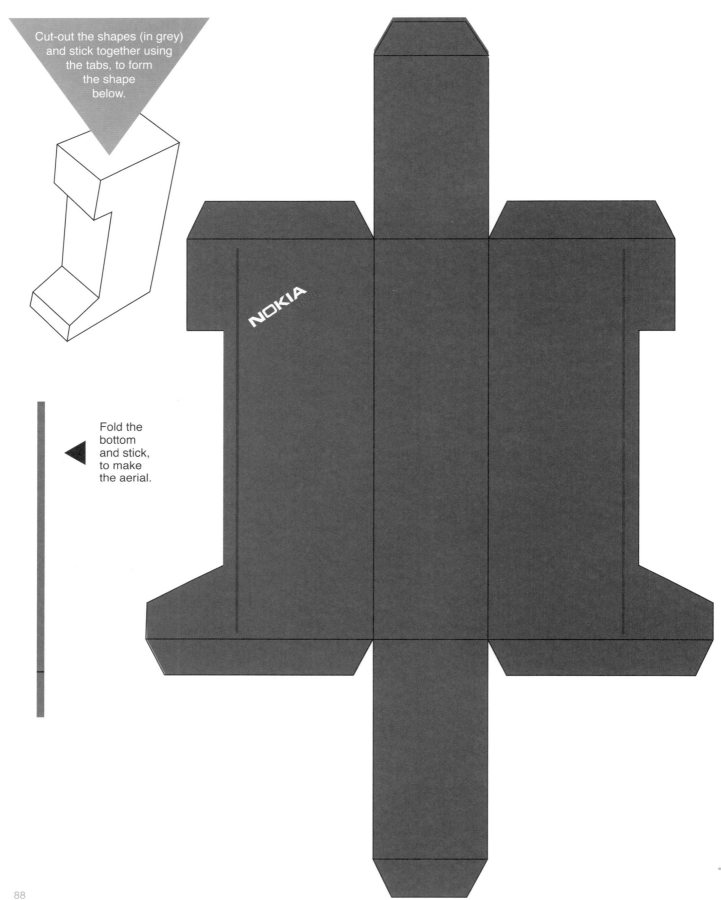

Cut-out the shapes (in grey) and stick together using the tabs, to form the shape below.

Fold the bottom and stick, to make the aerial.

NOKIA

88

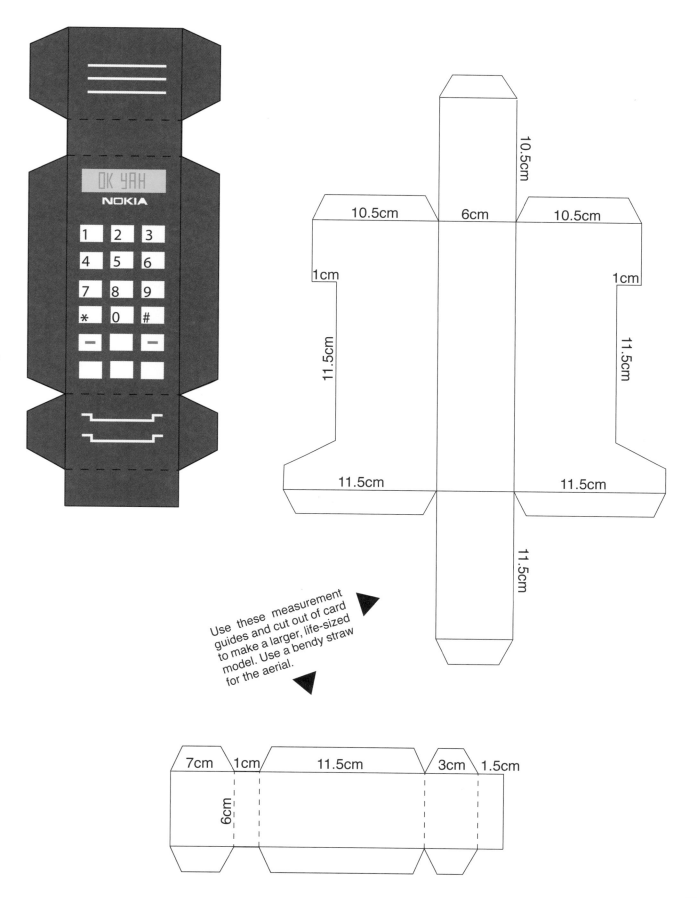

OK YAH

NOKIA

1	2	3
4	5	6
7	8	9
*	0	#

10.5cm

10.5cm   6cm   10.5cm

1cm   1cm

11.5cm

11.5cm

11.5cm   11.5cm

11.5cm

Use these measurement guides and cut out of card to make a larger, life-sized model. Use a bendy straw for the aerial.

| 7cm | 1cm | 11.5cm | 3cm | 1.5cm |

6cm

'80s DINNER PARTY

Throw your dinner guests back in time with a four course taste sensation. Put Prefab Sprout on the music centre, decorate the table with carnations, get out the best Eternal Beau and don't forget to use the hostess trolley!

Oooh Fancy Vol-au-vents for Hors d'oeuvres

STUFF YOU'LL NEED

425g packet of frozen puff pastry, thawed
1 egg, beaten
A 7.5-ish cm round pastry cutter
A 5-ish cm round pastry cutter

40g butter
40g flour
400ml hot milk
Salt-N-Pepa

100g cooked ham
2 tbsp finely grated parmesan

Roll out the pastry on a lightly floured surface and cut out 20–24 rounds using the cutter. Place these onto a lined baking sheet and then brush with the beaten egg.

Stamp circles (using the 7.5cm cutter) into your pastry rounds, without going all the way through.

Bake at 200°C for 10–15 minutes (or until risen and a golden brown colour). Let them cool down and then remove the centres with a sharp knife.

Melt the butter in a saucepan, stir in the flour and cook for two minutes on a low heat, stirring all the time.

Remove from the heat and gradually add the hot milk, whilst stirring ferociously. Return to the heat and carry on stirring, simmer for about five minutes.

Mix with the chopped ham and parmesan, put a small amount into each pastry casing and wow your guests with your fancyness.

I Melt With You
Modern English

Prawn Cocktail ... obviously

STUFF YOU'LL NEED

¼ kg shelled, prepared prawns
150ml thick mayonnaise
2 tsp lemon juice
15ml tomato purée
2 tsp Worcestershire sauce
Cayenne pepper
1 iceberg lettuce
4 slices of lemon
Brown bread
Butter
Salt-N-Pepa

Put the prawns into a large mixing bowl, then add the mayo, lemon juice, tomato purée, Worcestershire sauce and gently mix so that all the prawns are coated. Season with salt and pepper.

Finely shred the lettuce and divide equally between four serving glasses. Spoon in the mixture and sprinkle the top of each with a little cayenne pepper. Serve with a slice of lemon and brown bread and butter (cut into neat triangles).

Chicken Kiev, with Tossed Salad and Potato Croquettes

STUFF YOU'LL NEED

100g softened butter
Finely chopped parsely and chives
Clove of garlic, crushed
4 skinless chicken breasts, beaten thin
Plain flour for coating
1 egg, beaten
100g dried bread crumbs
Oil for deep-fat frying
4 slices of lemon

DRINK
Blue Nun,
Black Tower,
and
Advocaat

In a mixing bowl, beat the butter, lemon juice, parsley, chives and crushed garlic.

Lay the beaten chicken breasts flat and spoon some of the stuffing mix onto each one, rolling tightly so that the stuffing mix is completely enclosed.

Season some flour with salt and pepper and coat the chicken breasts in this. Dip into the beaten egg and completely cover in breadcrumbs.

Chill for at least one hour before frying.

Heat a deep fat fryer to 190ºC and then fry the chicken breasts, two at a time for 8–10 minutes, until crisp and golden.

Serve with shop-bought potato croquettes and salad. Garnish with a slice of lemon and a sprig of parsley for fancyness.

PLAY
'80s karaoke
games

Black Forest Gateaux

Buy a frozen Black Forest Gateau.
Thaw it out.
Serve on side plates decorated with paper doilies.

PLAY
*Trivial
Pursuit*

DRESS
Awesome!

DEBBIE GIBSON PAPER DOLL

Debbie Gibson shot to fame in 1987 with 'Only In My Dreams'. She was famous for singing, dancing, smiling and wearing a silly black hat.

Because she was enjoying superstardom at the same time as Tiffany, everyone assumed they were enemies, stealing each other's stone-washed denim jackets and scrunchies like they were going out of fashion. But they probably got along just fine. I actually felt a bit sorry for Tiffany because Debbie had her own synthesizer and computer at home whilst Tiffany was forced to sing in shopping centres.

Debbie should have appeared on Roy Castle's *Record Breakers* as, in 1988, at the tender age of 18, she was pronounced the youngest female to write, produce and perform a number one single ('Foolish Beat') ... and amazingly, she still holds that title today!

Fun Debbie Gibson Facts:
Debbie had a small, uncredited part in the 1984 film *Ghostbusters*.

In 2011, Debbie Gibson *and* Tiffany, starred together in sci-fi movie *Mega Python Vs Gataroid* (the sequel to the awesome *Mega Shark Vs Giant Octopus*).

Using spray adhesive, stick the paper doll, including the semi-circle stand, to a bit of card, an empty cereal packet will do. Then carefully cut around the doll figure using a craft knife or scissors. There's no need to stick the outfits onto card, just cut them out and then dress Debbie in whatever takes your fancy. I have included a blank Ra-Ra skirt for you to decorate with polka dots or simply colour in.

Electric Youth
Debbie Gibson

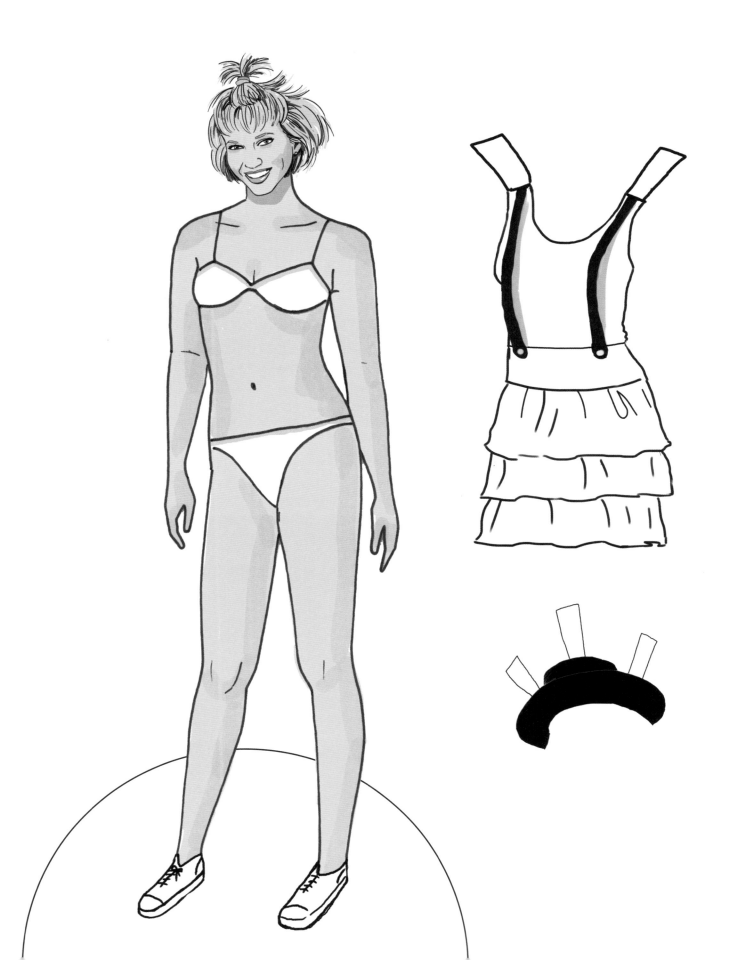

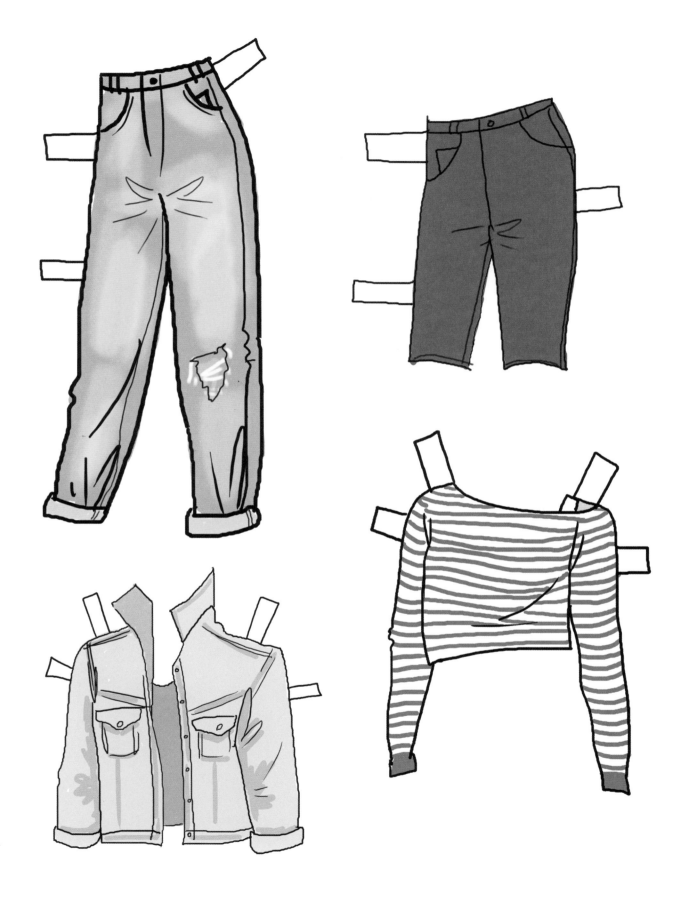

COLOUR IN NEIGHBOURS

New Sensation
INXS

SEQUINNED TOP

Want to look like a right bobby-dazzler?

Of course you do!

And you can, in this top, embellished with a 3-D glasses motif made out of sequins!

If you wear it down the local disco you'll be sure to attract the Ralph Macchio look-a-like of your dreams.

*Wild In
The Country*
Bow Wow Wow

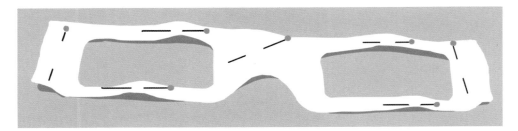

Cut out the template and attach to your sweatshirt with pins.

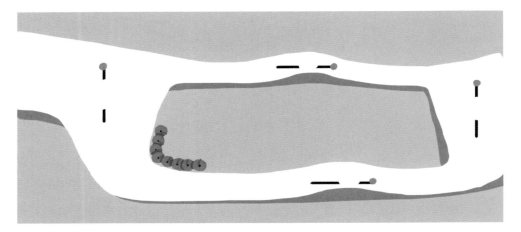

Starting with the lenses, sew on your sequins, overlapping them.

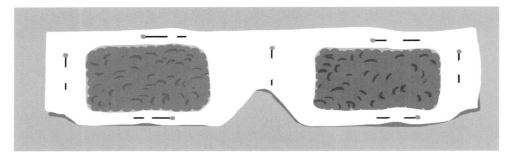

When you have filled in both the lenses draw around the template with tailor's chalk or a wash-off pen.

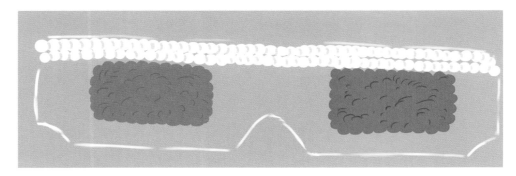

Using sequin strips, fill in the remainder.

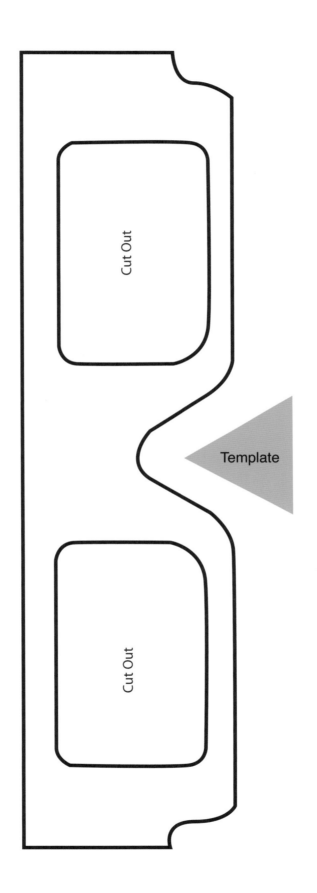

GUESS THE HAIR GAME!

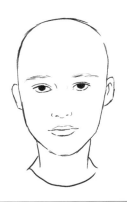

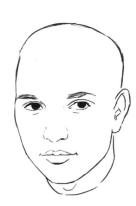

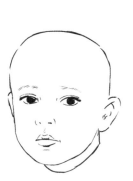

People had such funny hair in the '80s and we adored them for it! I remember my little sister begging my mum to let her have her hair like Wincey Willis from *TV:AM* and I'd have given my best glitter stretch jeans to have the hair sported by Emma from *Kate & Allie*. However, take away someone's hair and they're almost unrecognisable! See if you can match these silly '80s hair-dos to their celebrity heads ...

Love Plus One
Haircut 100

To make it easier, try cutting out the hair and placing it on the scalps!

PAPER PET SHOP BOYS

Being a somewhat naive child, I wanted to marry both the Pet Shop Boys. It was Chris Lowe who inspired me to get my own Casio synthesizer on which I learned how to play 'We All Stand Together'.

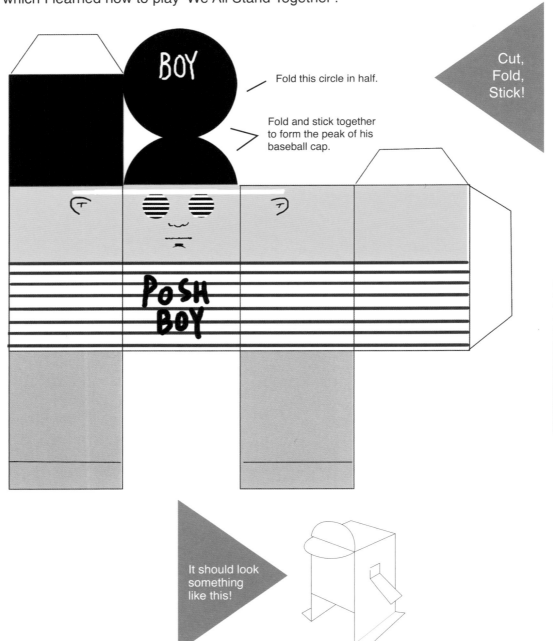

BOY

Fold this circle in half.

Fold and stick together to form the peak of his baseball cap.

Cut, Fold, Stick!

POSH BOY

It should look something like this!

It should look something like this!

Best Christmas No.1 ... ever!

Always On My Mind
Pet Shop Boys

DRAW IN 3-D

This cyan and magenta offset graph paper makes any black line drawing appear in 3-D with your new 3-D glasses on! Why don't you draw *E.T.*'s spaceship on here, then create your own '80s-inspired drawings on the next two pages!

The Story Of The Blues Part 1 **The Mighty Wah!**

MAKE YOUR OWN
3-D GLASSES

I went to see *Jaws 3-D* one Saturday with my dad and was amused at having to wear some silly cardboard glasses. My amusement soon waned when I almost soiled my Holly Hobby 'days of the week' pants (but being as disorganised as I am, I was probably wearing the wrong day anyway).

The sight of those huge teeth coming out of the screen and straight towards me was like something out of this world and I couldn't wait to tell everyone back at school (leaving out the bit about the pants, obviously).

Making your own '80s style 3-D glasses is incredibly simple! All you need is some card, a sheet of acetate or OHP film and two permanant markers, a red one and a blue one.

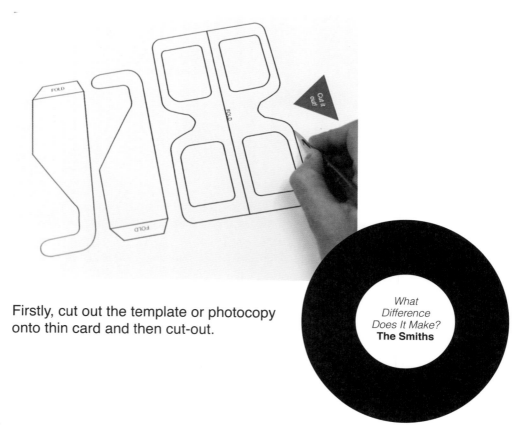

Firstly, cut out the template or photocopy onto thin card and then cut-out.

What Difference Does It Make? **The Smiths**

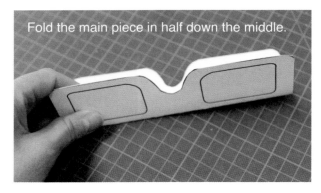
Fold the main piece in half down the middle.

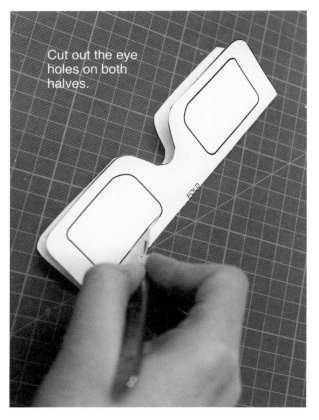
Cut out the eye holes on both halves.

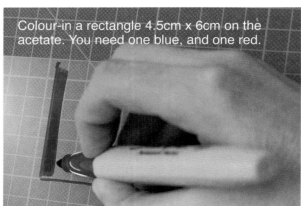
Colour-in a rectangle 4.5cm x 6cm on the acetate. You need one blue, and one red.

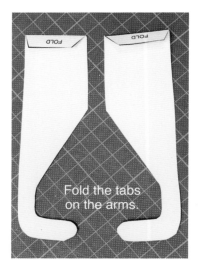
Fold the tabs on the arms.

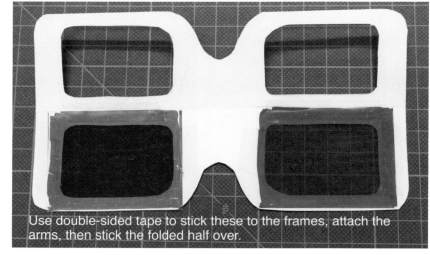
Use double-sided tape to stick these to the frames, attach the arms, then stick the folded half over.

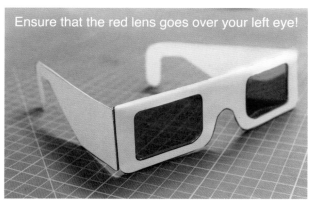
Ensure that the red lens goes over your left eye!

Now you can see 3-D stuff!

Test them on some 3-D test videos on YouTube!

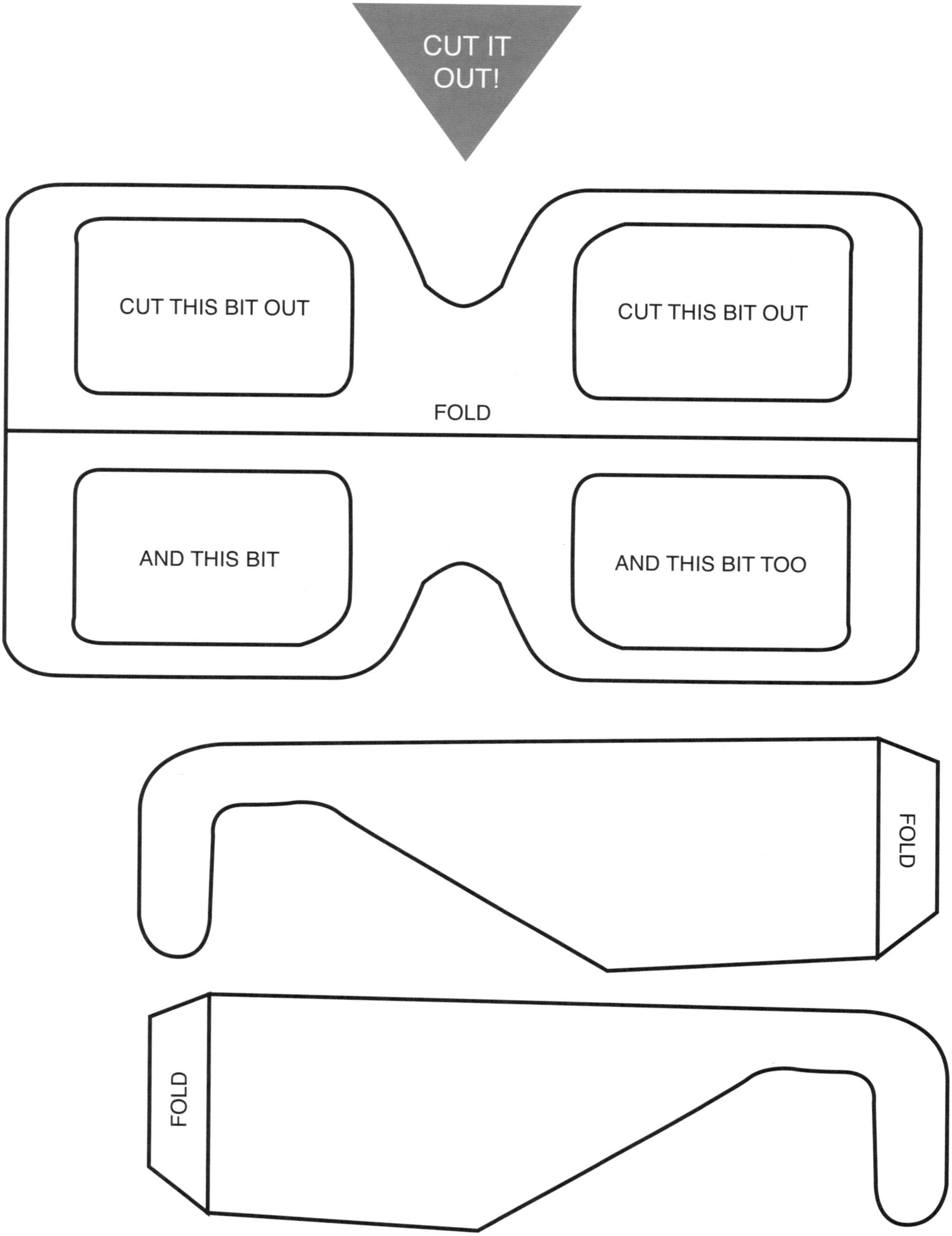

CUT IT OUT!

CUT THIS BIT OUT

CUT THIS BIT OUT

FOLD

AND THIS BIT

AND THIS BIT TOO

FOLD

FOLD

week 43

MARGARET THATCHER PORTRAIT & WALL STENCIL

Andy Warhol was, amongst other things, famous for his celebrity portraits, capturing the likes of Michael Jackson and Debbie Harry in the 1980s in his highly recognisable style. He sadly died in 1987.

Use bright colours!

Thriller
Michael Jackson

To create a Warhol-esque portrait of Margaret Thatcher, simply photocopy the wall stencil image onto acetate. Then paint on the back using poster paints or acrylics.

Start with the whites of the eyes, then eyeshadow, facial shadow, hair and then flesh.

To use as a
wall stencil, follow
the instructions
or Week 23.

FINGER-KNIT A SNOOD

The 'snood', which has recently made a comeback, is a woolly tube that you can put around your neck like a scarf *or* (and this is the clever bit), pull it up onto your head like a coat hood should it get a bit nippy out. Nik Kershaw used to wear one and it made him look all sultry, but don't let that put you off.

This knitting pattern is great because it is as easy as the *Superman* dance routine and requires no knitting needles. All you need is a ball of wool and two hands (with most fingers still attached).

So, here goes ...

1

To 'cast on', place the end of the wool between your thumb and your index finger and then weave it around the other fingers.

Go around your little finger and then weave back again to and around your index finger.

The Riddle
Nik Kershaw

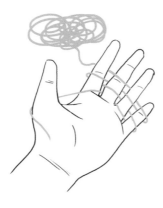

2

Do the same again, weave through to and around your little finger and then back to your index finger.

There should now be two loops on each finger.

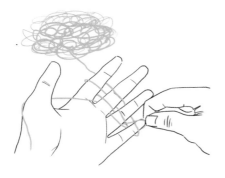

3

Starting with your little finger, pull the bottom loop up and over the top loop so that the bottom loop is now behind the finger and the top loop is still in front.

Working from right to left, do this with the remaining fingers, finishing with the index finger.

You should now have just one loop on each finger and some knotted business going on at the back.

4

Take the wool on its woven trip to your little finger and then back to your index finger again.

Starting with the little finger, pull the bottom loops up and over again and repeat this process again and again.

5 It will not be long before you witness something that looks like knitting going on round the back! Congratulations!

6 Should you need to go for a dance, the toilet or for a little nap, carefully pull the loop off of each finger and thread a pencil or pen through the loops for sakekeeping.

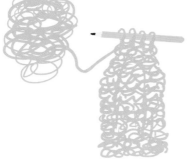

7 Continue, until your length of knitting measures around 7m.

8 Once you have reached the required length, you will need to 'cast off'. To do this, take the loop from your little finger, and place it over your wedding ring finger, then take the bottom loop from your ring finger, bring it over the top loop and place onto the middle finger. Repeat this process for the middle and your index finger until only your index finger has a loop on it. Cut off from your length of wool, thread this through your remaining loop and pull tight.

9 Once you have your length and have 'cast off', you can now start to coil it around and, with your wool (no needle necessary), sew the coil together by threading the wool in and out of the edging loops. Make the neck as tight or as loose as you desire ... and just like that, you are now the proud owner of a snood. Put it on and look all moody.

STITCHIN'-BY-NUMBERS

Using the same cross-stitching technique as in Week 8, create a pixelated portrait of Michael J. Fox.

Using one cross per square on the grid, your image portrait will measure approximately 8 x 7cm.

For a larger image, multiply each number by four, so if the grid shows this ...

... you would actually, sew this.

7	7	7	7
7	7	7	7
6	6	4	4
6	6	4	4

The numbers on the grid relate to the following Anchor cross-stitch threads:

1	=	00882
2	=	347
3	=	883
4	=	884
5	=	351
6	=	1050
7	=	381
8	=	380
9	=	121
10	=	273
11	=	130

For the background (shaded in beige), you can leave blank, or use a shade of beige/grey of your choice.

She Bop
Cyndi Lauper

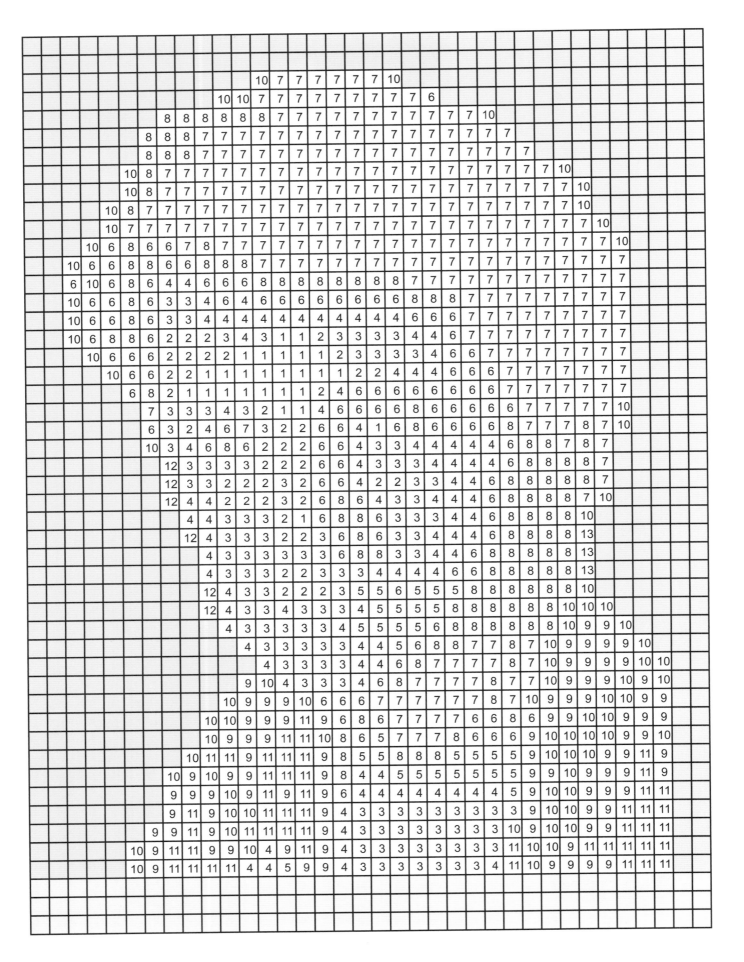

MICHAEL J. FOX
PAPER DOLL

Before *Back To The Future* was released in 1985, my bedroom walls only had eyes for Shakin' Stevens, but then POW! My 12-year-old heart was stolen by a cute American boy wearing a red body warmer and riding a skateboard. Forever the trendsetter, I was wearing a red body warmer long before Michael J. Fox was, it's just that mine had the words *Shakin'* and *Stevens* embroidered on the back by my talented mum (And mum, by the way, there are just some things you should not do for your children no matter how much they beg you!).

So, down came Shaky and up went Michael J. Fox, lovingly cut out of *Look In* and *Smash Hits* magazine. Just hearing the Huey Lewis and the News song made me come over all funny and practice my snogging technique upon my increasingly soggy wall posters, my sister's Care Bears blushing in the background.

Back To The Future was a huge success that lead to a trilogy and, luckily for me and my bedroom walls, Michael J. Fox became one of the biggest stars of the decade, also starring in *Teen Wolf* and *The Secret of My Success* (a film which contains some of the best '80s hair-dos you'll witness) amongst many, many others.

Using spray adhesive, stick the paper doll, including the semi-circle stand, to a bit of card, an empty cereal packet will do. Then carefully cut around the doll figure using a craft knife or scissors. There's no need to stick the outfits onto card, just cut them out and then dress Michael in whatever takes your fancy. I have included a blank T-Shirt for you to add your own design or slogan onto ... or you could just leave it white, for that 'Nick Kamen in the laundrette' look.

Here Comes Your Man
The Pixies

CASSETTE CARD

Cut out a piece of card
10 x 6.5cm.

Cut another piece 7x1.5cm
then cut off the corners to
make this shape.

Using a different colour,
cut a 9 x 4cm rectangle, then cut
a 6 x1.5cm section, out of it.

*Walk Out
To Winter*
Aztec Camera

Cut out the
strip below
to write your
message
on it!

A

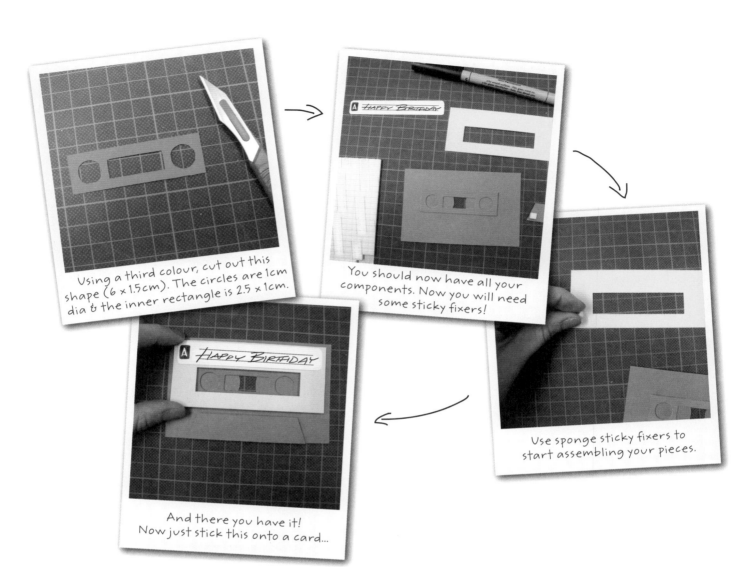

Using a third colour, cut out this shape (6 x 1.5cm). The circles are 1cm dia & the inner rectangle is 2.5 x 1cm.

You should now have all your components. Now you will need some sticky fixers!

Use sponge sticky fixers to start assembling your pieces.

And there you have it! Now just stick this onto a card...

Use gold and glittery card to make a Christmas version!

ANOTHER SLOGAN T-SHIRT

Jim'll Fix It was to Saturday teatimes what Rod Hull was to Emu and it was the perfect build up before *The Fall Guy*.

The excitement experienced whilst waiting to see what crazy antics someone was going to get up to, was almost unbearable ... and then some kid would waste their opportunity by visiting a glass factory or suchlike. Plonkers!

It wasn't always glass factories though, sometimes they sang backing vocals for their favourite pop star and if you don't know about the packed lunch on the rollercoaster then you haven't lived.

Every lucky 'fixee' got to snuggle up to Jim and receive their medallion. However if, like me, you weren't that lucky, you can quietly protest with this slogan T-Shirt.

Follow the same instruction as Week 11.

Reward
The Teardrop Explodes

JIM DIDN'T

FIT IT

FIX FOR

ME ME

POP-UP VALENTINE'S CARD

Love is in the air and here is your chance to S.W.A.L.K. your way into someone's heart ...

Forever.

During my teenage years, I had begun to accept that my love for Michael J. Fox and Chris Lowe from the Pet Shop Boys, was unlikely to be requited. I had realised that if I ever were to be married (in the dress I had chosen in BHS one Saturday while my grandma returned some pop-socks) I would have to choose *normal* boys and write their full name, followed my mine, and then cross out the letters as I chanted some magic spell about European cattle. Inevitably, they always ended in either 'friendship' or 'courtship' and so had to watch, green-eyed and lonely as seemingly *everyone* cavorted upon my TV screen. Zammo and Jackie in *Grange Hill,* Maddie and David in *Moonlighting,* Penny and Vincent in *Just Good Friends*, not to mention Ian and little Jeanette Krankie, EVEN ROLAND FROM *GRANGE HILL* WAS GETTING IT ON!

Well, you'll be relieved to hear that I did find love in the end and he'll definitely be getting one of these mega-romantic Valentine's cards.

There are four designs to choose from and you'll need a piece of A5 card, folded in half, lengthways (so it makes a postcard-sized card). You can buy card, this size, already scored and folded, in many colours, and with matching envelopes. However, making your own is easy, just score the card with the back of your craft knife before creasing.

Don't Talk To Me About Love
Altered Images

I **LOVE** *you* **MORE** **than...**

1

Cut around these words and stick them haphazardly upon the front of your card. You could use foam sticky fixers if you'd like them raised.

2

Cut out your chosen heart (see overleaf) and fold down the middle, so that the image is inside.

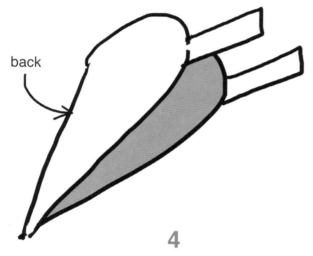

back

3

Fold the tabs backwards and attach double-sided tape to them.

double-sided tape

4

Place the folded heart inside the opened card like so and close the card so that the tabs stick inside the card.

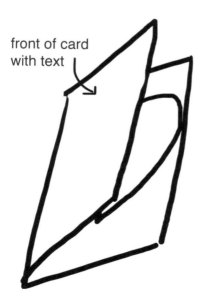

front of card with text

5

Tah-Dah! Your card is finished and awaiting the lucky recipient!

PAINTING-BY-NUMBERS

Mud = M

Red = R

Pink = P

Flesh = F

Light Brown = LB

Brown = B

Blonde = BL

White = Left Blank

During the late seventies and early eighties, Debbie Harry was adored by men and admired by women ... and she still is! You wouldn't catch Miss Harry wearing a red body warmer with 'Shakin' Stevens' on the back! Oh no. She had more cool in her little finger than Denise Huxtable had in her whole body and people just couldn't get enough. My painting-by-numbers drawing of Debbie Harry, is based on a Polaroid photograph taken by Andy Warhol in 1980.

Simply use the colour guide on the right to paint the image on the following page (or download an un-numbered version from www.80sbumperbook.com).

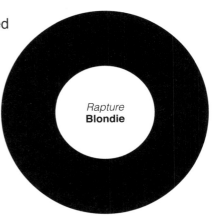

Rapture
Blondie

COLOURING IN

Yes We Know It's Christmas!

END OF THE DECADE QUIZ

1. In 1982, East End gangsters, Ronnie and Reggie Kray, were let out of prison for one day, what was the reason?
2. What was the highest grossing film of the decade?
3. In which year did the £1 note, cease to exist as legal tender in England?
4. Which single did Madonna perform at the first MTV Video Music Awards in 1985?
5. In 1981, what was the first music video to be shown on MTV?
6. Who was the first to sing on Band Aid's 'Do They Know It's Christmas?'
7. Which Simple Minds song became the theme to *The Breakfast Club?*
8. Who shot J.R.?
9. If Tom Cruise is Maverick, who is *Iceman*?
10. Name the four *Golden Girls?* (First names will do.)
11. Name all five members of *New Kids On The Block*? (First names will do.)
12. What was Mork's trademark catchphrase in *Mork & Mindy*?
13. Which British band covered 'People Are Strange' by The Doors, in the '80s?
14. In which UK sitcom featured the characters, Linda, David, Robert and Amy, and the San Remo hotel in Marbella?
15. ... and which actor played David?
16. Which '80s girl band was fronted by Susanna Hoff?
17. Name *The Cosby Show* spin-off that premiered in 1987?
18. Eddie 'The Eagle' Edwards failed to win any medals at which Winter Olympics? (Year and place)
19. Which 1985 film saw two teenage nerds 'create' a woman using their computer programming skills?
20. ... and which actress played their creation?

Dancing With Myself
Generation X

21. Who is this devilishly handsome chap?

22. Name the hunk.

23. Name the series.

24. Name the puff-ball wearers.

25. In the early 1980s, who was assistant editor at *Smash Hits* magazine, until he found fame as one half of Britain's best loved pop duos?
26. Who was Zola Budd's arch enemy during the 1984, Los Angeles Olympics?
27. Who was Roland Rat's leek loving friend?
28. Presenters of the *Wide Awake Club* were Timmy Mallet, Michaela Strachan and who else?
29. Which playful gadget, released in Japan in 1989, was created by Gunpei Yokoi?
30. Who played Bud Fox's father in the 1987 film, *Wall Street*?

Match the name on the left, to the artist on the right!

What's your score?

Frankie	Michael Jackson
Jennifer	Sister Sledge
Robert De Niro	Dexy's Midnight Runners
Eloise	Kool & the Gang
Veronica	Europe
Carrie	Elvis Costello
Joanna	The Damned
Gloria	Lloyd Cole & The Commotions
Diana	Laura Branigan
Eileen	Bananarama

/40

Answers on page 141

THE HISTORY BIT

Okay, so some of you you may not get all the points of reference in this book, or you may have kids who are asking you questions. Or you may have simply forgotten! So, here is an explanation of some of the references in the book:

Bagsy That is a game where you take one of those big, mail order catalogues and, with a sibling, turn the pages quickly one by one, bashing your hand firmly on the item on that page that you would like the most and shouting out before anyone else. It's a great game but it does get a bit tedious during the fishing equipment or clothes airers sections.

Denise Huxtable was a character in 'The Cosby Show' (1984-1992). Heathcliffe Huxtable was a doctor and lived in a massive house in New York with his wife and four children. Denise was his cool daughter, played by Lisa Bonet, and every girl in school at the time wanted to be her. She was wearing Harem trousers 25 years before anyone else even knew about them!

A **TDK90** was a blank cassette tape you could fill with a whole 90 minutes of music! Father Christmas used to bring packs of five, until video recorders came out and then he would bring blank VHS tapes instead (which if you 'long play', you could record the whole of the *Brookside Omnibus* on a Saturday).

Brookside was Channel 4's first soap and was shown on their opening night of 2nd November 1982. It was a very exciting evening as there were only three other channels, and had been for yonks! *Brookside* was set in a suburb of Liverpool and featured a new build estate where chavs and middle-class yuppies lived in perfect harmony.

'Pong' was a really cool arcade game. It featured a black screen, two white sticks and a ball that was supposed to replicate a game of table tennis. It was absolutely brilliant and you can now get Atari's 'Greatest Hits' iPhone/Ipad App which includes 'Pong'.

AWESOME!

Live It Up
Mental As Anything

RADICAL!

When the 'Space Invaders' arcade game was released in 1978, there was an immediate national shortage of 100 Yen coins in Japan. In the game, you had to shoot a pixelated alien enemy and this is on the aforementioned Atari App too.

'You Drive Me Crazy' was a No.2 UK hit for Shakin' Stevens in 1980. It reached No.1 in Ireland and No.2 in New Zealand and is definitely one of the greatest songs of all time ... ever!

George Michael and Andrew Rigley formed WHAM! after meeting at school in Bushey, Watford. In America they were known as *Wham! UK* due to a naming conflict with an American band (I don't know what they were called though). Wham! sold 25 million records between 1982 and 1986 and their first UK single 'Wham! Rap' was the first British chart single to feature rapping. Their backing singers, Pepsi and Shirlie went AWOL and had their own string of hits, starting with 'Heartache' in 1986.

The Valentine's card couples are Damon & Debbie (a teenage couple from *Brookside* who had their own spin-off show where Damon got stabbed on a bridge in York). Rocky & Adrian (from the *Rocky* films) where Sylvester Stallone plays a boxer who runs up some steps because the whole neighbourhood was chasing him. Jonathan & Jennifer (from *Hart to Hart*) act the story of a handsome couple, played handsomely by Robert Wagner and Stefanie Powers. They solved crimes, along with their Butler, Max, and their dog, Freeway. Scott & Charlene had one of the best weddings of the decade in the Australian soap, *Neighbours.*

Diff'rent Strokes was a comedy series that ran from 1978-1986. It featured a rich, Manhattan widower who adopts the children of his late African/American maid. Arnold was played by the brilliant Gary Coleman who sadly died in 2010.

'Nobody Puts Baby In The Corner' was one of the most memrable film quotes from the decade. It came from the film *Dirty Dancing* starring the late Patrick Swayze and Jennifer Grey. It is a film about a guy who teaches a young girl to walk on a log, successfully.

Ferris Bueller was the lead charcter from the John Hughes film *Ferris Bueller's Day Off,* about a teenage boy who takes the day off school and persuades his girlfriend Sloane, and best pal, Cameron, to join him. Ferris basically thinks he's it. John Hughes was responsible for the decade's best films (*The Breakfast Club, Sixteen Candles, Pretty In Pink, Werd Science*) and had an amazing talent for connecting with teenagers.

Margaret Thatcher was the first female Prime Minister of Great Britain and ruled from 1979-1990. Being from the small, mining town of Barnsley, I am forced to despise her and I still have nightmares about the 'Free School Meals' queue being too long during the Miner's Strike (1984-1985).

Grange Hill was a BBC TV series by Phil Redmond of *Brookside* and *Hollyoaks* fame. It was set at a secondary school in London and ran from 1978-2008. Zammo was a heroin addicted character played by Lee MacDonald. His girlfriend Jackie, and her mate Faye (who knew a good dance routine) were so worried about him that they performed a song entitled 'Just Say No', hoping that he would stop taking drugs. It was a huge hit in 1986. I don't remember if he stopped taking drugs.

The **Lamborghini Countach** was produced between 1974 and 1990. The word 'countach', in Italian, is a term of astonishment, usually when a man sees a beautiful woman. **Jaws 3D** was *not* directed by Steven Spielberg, but by Joe Alves. Dennis Quaid starred as Mike Brody (son of Chief Brody from Jaws 1 & 2) who has a few minor hiccups when a 35ft shark becomes trapped in the Seaworld Theme Park. The shark eats some people and Dennis Quaid goes on to star as Lindsay Lohan's dad in *The Parent Trap*.

E.T. was directed by Steven Spielberg and was the sad tale of Elliott, a young boy from the suburbs, who finds a lost alien who nearly dies in a tent. But he goes home in the end so it's all okay. However, everyone cries anyway.

Madonna is the pop-star who just keeps on giving. She has released a staggering 77 singles so far, starting with 'Everybody' in 1982.

The **Etch-A-Sketch** was invented by Frenchman André Cassagnes and has been hailed 'one of the best creative toys of the twentieth century'. Ooh La La!

Bananarama consisted of Keren Woodward, Sara Dallin and Siobhan Fahey. They shot to fame with 'Really Saying Something' in 1982 and duetted with Lananeeneenoonoo (French & Saunders) on 'Help' for Comic Relief in 1988.

Bros were twin brothers, Matt and Luke Goss, and Craig Logan. They were managed by Tom Watkins of The Pet Shop Boys and East 17 fame and they were HUGE ... for a short time. If you listen to their version of 'Silent Night' from 1988 you will agree that Matt Goss started the trend for 'over-singing'.

Stock, Aitken & Waterman were a songwriting and producing team that sold 40 million records. They were partly responsible for 13 number ones in the 1980s:

'You Spin Me Round' – Dead Or Alive, 1985
'Respectable' – Mel & Kim, 1987
'Let It Be' – FerryAid, 1987 (Zeebrugge Disaster Fund)
'Never Gonna Give You Up' – Rick Astely, 1987
'I Should Be So Lucky' – Kylie Minogue, 1987
'Especially For You' – Kylie & Jason, 1989
'Too Many Broken Hearts' – Jason Donovan, 1989
'Hand On Your Heart' – Kylie Minogue, 1989
'Ferry 'Cross the Mersey'– Various, 1989
        (Hillsborough Disaster Fund)
'Sealed With A Kiss' – Jason Donovan, 1989
'You'll Never Stop Me From Loving You' – Sonia, 1989
'Do They Know It's Christmas?' – Band Aid, 1989

They also had hits with Big Fun, Hazell Dean, Mandy Smith (of Bill Wyman fame), Pat (Sharp) & Mick, Sinitta (Simon Cowell's BFF), Samantha Fox, The Reynolds Girls and Roland Rat.

RUN DMC and Aerosmith had a massive hit with the rock v rap breakthrough combination, 'Walk This Way' in 1986.

Jim'll Fix It ran on the BBC between 1975 and 1994. This Saturday teatime show saw children write in to have Jimmy Savill make their dreams come true on national television. The brilliant theme tune was recorded by the Wee Papa Girl Rappas who went on to have a hit with 'Wee Rule', in 1988.

Risky Business was a 1983 film starring a young Tom Cruise as Joel Goodsen. In a nut-shell, his mum and dad went on holiday so he put on some Ray-Bans and had a good time ... with a prostitute, played by Rebecca De Mornay.

Neighbours, the Australian soap that stomped all over *Sons & Daughters,* was set in the fictional town of Erinsborough and focussed upon the residents of Ramsay Street. It started in 1985 and was a huge UK hit for the BBC with an amazing 20 million people watching Scott & Charlene's wedding. It was on weekdays at 1:30pm and then repeated at 5:35pm. It took a bit of a down-turn when students realised that they were going to leave university one day and that they should probably get out of bed and do some studying so that it wasn't a complete waste of money.

The Fall Guy ran from 1981 to 1986 and was the light-hearted tale of Colt Seavers, a Hollywood stunt-man who did a spot of bounty-hunting when work was slow. He had some chums called Howie and Jodie and they would commonly frolic in their outdoor hot-tub together.

'**Last Christmas**' was a 1984 Christmas No.2 hit for Wham!

'**A Winter's Tale**' was a 1982 Christmas No. 2 hit for David Essex.

'**Merry Christmas Everyone**' was a 1985 Christmas No.1 hit for Shakin' Stevens (get in there Shaky!)

The Pet Shop Boys are the most succesful duo in UK history. Since 1986, they have had 42, top 30 singles and 4 No.1 hits.

It Aint What You Do
Fun Boy Three & Bananarama

WHAT TO BUY, WHERE TO BUY IT

Basic Kit: Craft knife, Cutting mat, Double-sided tape and Spray adhesive

FELT TIPS FOR COLOURING-IN

You can buy quite nice brush-tipped pens from many supermarkets for £2-3 and these are okay. If, like me, you take your colouring in more seriously, I recommend Letraset ProMarkers as a fairly inexpensive professional marker (around £6-8 for a pack of 5). You'll be amazed what a difference, decent pens and colours make to your images! You can get these from Letraset.com as well as most art stores.

POST-IT NOTES

You can get these in any Supermarket but for packs of really bright colours you may have to go to a large stationary store or online.

AIR DRY CLAY

I use a product called Sculpt Dry in Terracotta, and you can get this from most arts/crafts stores for around £4.

CAKE MAKING

You can get most ingredients from your local supermarket, but the colured blocks of sugar paste may have to be bought from a specialist cake decorators or large craft store.

FABRIC SPRAY PAINT & T SHIRTS

I used Simply Spray and you can get this for about £4 from art and craft stores, or from simplyspray.com.
Many high street discount fashion stores and department stores sell cheap white T-Shirts. Eighties fashion was baggy and loose and Men's Mediums were used for the examples in this book.

GUITAR

I suggest you borrow one, and if you are buying your first, do get advice from someone who plays.

You can get some great second-hand ones so check out eBay, your local charity shops and even car boot sales. You may be best starting with a junior model until your fingers get used to all the stretching.

CROSS-STITCH, APPLIQUE, SEQUINS & TIE

Anchor threads were used for the cross-stitch projects, along with 14-count canvas. You can get these from most haberdasheries or craft shops along with iron-on adhesive and iron-on interfacing, cotton threads, sequins etc.

PLAIN CANVAS BAGS

These cost around £2 from larger craft stores, however if you want to do a few as gifts, do shop around on the internet, as buying in bulk will get your cost down to just a few pence per bag!

LEGO

Large toy stores will sell Lego but it's not cheap. I recommend that you get your grey board from there but check out eBay for second hand bag-loads of bricks!

LAZERTRAN CERAMIC TRANSFER PAPER & TATTOO PAPER

Lazertran.com sell this in A4 or A3 sized sheets and for laser or inkjet printers. It costs around £12 for 8 A4 sheets, but it has so many uses that it will really inspire you. You can buy a different type of ceramic transfer paper from www.craftycomputerpaper.com and you can also get the tattoo transfer paper here. Do make sure you order the correct type for your printer!

WALL SPRAY PAINT

Try www.graff-city.com where it will cost you around £5 for a large black can.

GUESS THE HAIR GAME!

CYNDI LAUPER

LIMAHL

BOY GEORGE

DREW BARRYMORE

PRINCE

TIFFANY

RALPH MACCHIO

MARGARET THATCHER

END OF THE DECADE QUIZ

1. To attend their mum's funeral
2. *E.T.*
3. 1988
4. 'Like A Virgin'
5. 'Video Killed The Radio Star' by Buggles
6. Paul Young
7. 'Don't You Forget About Me'
8. Kristin Shepard
9. Val Kilmer
10. Sophia, Blanche, Rose, Dorothy
11. Jordan, Jonathan, Joey, Donnie & Danny
12. Nanoo Nanoo
13. Echo & The Bunnymen
14. Duty Free
15. Keith Barron
16. The Bangles
17. *A Different World*
18. Calgary, 1988
19. *Weird Science*
20. Kelly LeBrock

21. Rick Astley
22. Matt Dillon
23. *Moonlighting*
24. Pepsi & Shirlie
25. Neil Tennant (of the Pet Shop Boys)
26. Mary Decker
27. Errol (the hamster)
28. Tommy Boyd
29. Nintendo Gameboy
30. Martin Sheen
31. Sister Sledge – Frankie
32. Lloyd Cole – Jennifer
33. Bananarama – Robert De Niro
34. Elvis Costello – Veronica
35. Europe – Carrie
36. Kool & The Gang – Joanna
37. Laura Branigan – Gloria
38. Michael Jackson – Diana
39. The Damned – Eloise
40. Dexy's Midnight Runners – Eileen

DEDICATION'S WHAT YOU NEED

For my three brilliant children, George, Charlie and Pearl

I can't begin my thanks and dedications without first mentioning the late, great Roy Castle now can I? Or Bob Holness, Gary Coleman, Rod Hull, Jimmy Savile, Patrick Swayze, John Hughes and, of course, Tony Hart. Without you, my '80s childhood would not have been half of what it was.

Thank you Alicia Armstrong for all your help, whether it was cross-stitching until your fingers bled, running around with cassette tapes at the drop of a hat, helping me attach balloons to my son or back-combing your daughter's hair to within an inch of it's life. I appreciated it all. You are a true friend.

To Andie Jackman for the ace Pac-Man cake (thecupcakebaker.co.uk)

To my wonderful teenage models, my son George Blessed and Phoebe Armstrong. You were both moody, professional and totally rad! And to my two very talented creative helpers, Jack Booth (jack-booth.co.uk) and Francine Green (gloriasbeard.blogspot.com). You'll both go far!

To Eve and Richard, you life-changers you!

To Abi Jackson, sewer extraordinaire! (abijackson.com)

And to all my fab Facebook friends who have showered me with '80s memories whenever I 'virtually' asked them to!

But, most of all, thank you to my mum Linda and my husband Andy. I could not do any of this without your overwhelming support. Without you I honestly don't know where I'd be.

Photographs by Jack Booth, Francine Green and Mel Elliott. Photographs on p.134 by All Star Pics.

ABOUT '80s MEL

HOME

A modern detached house with my Mum, Linda and younger sister, Nanette, in Barnsley, South Yorkshire. We lived on a cul-de-sac that had a great un-kept bit of land to the back where rhubarb grew in abundance and where a set of corrugated metal garages stood. These were great for hiding in between when the witch came out (every street had a witch in the '80s).

I would constantly play out in my 'hood with my friends Rachel Markey and Tina Mathers. There was a street called Hartington Drive where the 'rough kids' lived. We had to make the terrifying journey across this street to get to our 'den' (a weeping willow tree) every day during the big holidays. I still shudder, just thinking about it.

HOBBIES

Cliché I know, but I have been drawing since I was little. On paper, walls, sofas, you name it. I would often sit there, bored with a pencil and paper complaining to my Mum that 'I don't know what to draw!', until my Mum bought me a brilliant book entitled *What Shall We Draw?* and then I was off and away!

I also used to race grasstrack motorbikes until I was about 10 (when I just wanted to fit in) and fell in love with my main rival, Martin Jones. I don't think I ever spoke to him though.

MUSIC

Shaky. Just Shaky!

FILM

All the usual blockbusters, and on Saturdays, round at my dad's, we would get pop and crisps and watch films inside the video rental shop.

TOY

Nintendo Game & Watch – yes it was a watch *and* a game! (no camera or phone or calendar or anything else though). I also loved my fashion wheel that was a Christmas present from my Auntie Sheila.

TV

Minipops, The Fall Guy, Brookside, Blockbusters, Neighbours, The Littlest Hobo, all the great stuff.

ABOUT MEL NOW

Mel currently lives in Hastings with her husband and three children, where they are referred to by neighbours as 'that mental family with all the cats who sing too loudly to Spandau Ballet'.

Mel spends much of her time in her studio down the road, illustrating her colouring books and paper dolls, as well as magazine and newspaper comissions. Her love of glossy magazines, fashion, interiors, celebrity and all things pop culture, influence her work enormously, and with her gouache paintings, she strives for perfection in an attempt to mimic the magazine images she leafs through, day in, day out.

Mel dreams of one day living in LA and hopes that her business, 'I Love Mel', loves her enough to fund it.

Nanette and Me

Me on a motorbike

All scrubbed up and wearing a dress